P9-CEY-700

# Chopper! Chopper!

# Chopper! Chopper!

## Poetry from Bordered Lives

## VERÓNICA REYES

ARKTOI BOOKS | *Pasadena, CA*

*Chopper! Chopper! Poetry from Bordered Lives*
Copyright © 2013 by Verónica Reyes
All Rights Reserved

No part of this book may be used or reproduced in any manner whatsoever without the prior written permission of both the publisher and the copyright owner.

Book layout and design by Aly Owen & Jaimie Evans

Library of Congress Cataloging-in-Publication Data

Reyes, Verónica.
  Chopper! chopper! : poetry from bordered lives / Verónica Reyes.
    pages cm
  ISBN 978-0-9890361-0-8
  1.  Mexican Americans—Poetry. 2.  Lesbians—Poetry. 3.  East Los Angeles (Calif.)—Poetry. 4.  El Paso (Tex.)—Poetry.  I. Title.
  PS3620.E939C48 2013
  811'.6—dc23
                        2013007297

The Los Angeles County Arts Commission, the National Endowment for the Arts, the City of Pasadena Cultural Affairs Division, Sony Pictures Entertainment, the Los Angeles Department of Cultural Affairs, and the Dwight Stuart Youth Fund partially support Red Hen Press.

First Edition
Published by Arktoi Books
An imprint of Red Hen Press
www.arktoi.com
www.redhen.org

# Gracias and Acknowledgments

After many years of hard work, struggle, and perseverance, this book has come to life. I am proud of this work. These poems emerged from the barrio, my corazón, my dreams, my realities, my homes, and beautiful energies beyond the calles of East L.A. They are me and reflect the barrio life from where I'm from. On this long poet's road, there was pain, cariño, sacrifice, and joy in creating these poems.

Throughout these years, there have been significant friends who merit gracias for all their layers of support. To Wanda and Cindy, my deepest thank you for the moral, emotional, and sometimes economic support during the early years when it was tough, lonely, and you know the rest. To Lynn, from our grad school years to present, thank you for being there and for our poetic friendship. To Cristina, thank you for believing in me, tú sabes.

To my familia, thank you for being a great source of inspiration for my poetry. There are too many names to list, but gracias for my jota poet support. And gracias to the mujeres de MALCS for the early years and for the space to share my poetry. In Toronto, I was fortunate to cross paths with many wonderful Canadians—thank you for the friendships and cheering Chicana jota poetry. To Brenda, my butch buddy, bueno, thank you for your friendship and making Toronto a beautiful and fun maple leaf city to live in.

And a muy deep cariño thank you to Claudia Borgna, my partner, for all the layers of support, love, and more throughout these past few years.

To Eloise, my editor/publisher, thank you for trusting in this manuscript knowing that the language and stories crossed borders from el barrio to academia. For believing this type of scripted poetry needs to be published and heard in the literary communities and beyond.

Over the years, many people, friends crossed my poet's life in East L.A., Long Beach, El Paso, and Toronto. Gracias to all who shared words of encouragement, whether at a poetry reading, a coffee joint, on the calles, a university/college campus, or at a bus stop. Gracias to the gente of North Sydney Drive, East L.A. Gracias for the poetry.

Many thanks to the editors of the following journals in which these poems first appeared: *Borderlands: Texas Poetry Review*, "Texas Twilight on the Border (El Paso, TX)"; *Feminist Studies*, "Chopper! Chopper!"; *The Gay & Lesbian Review*, "Praise the Word: Audre Lorde is Still Alive!"; *The New York Quarterly*, "Winter Desert/Summer Glacier"; *North American Review*, "The Queer Retablo Series: Butch-Femme Dialogue"; *Northridge Review*, "Los Angeles River—Río Grande: brown-speckled mirrors" as "Los Angeles-El Paso Rivers: brown-speckled mirrors"; *Río Grande Review*, "Theoretical Discourse over 'Sopa' (what does it mean?)"; *Willow Springs*, "El Diablo"; and *ZYZZYVA*, "Cholo Lessons por Vida."

Note that "El Diablo" was the winner for AWP's Intro-Journal Project. "Marimacha," "El Bus," "Praise the Word: Audre Lorde is Still Alive!" and "Panocha Power!" have appeared in the JOTA zines. Finally, a few poems were written at Vermont Studio Center and Napa Valley Writers' Conference.

I would also like to thank these writers/performers for the opportunity to inscribe their lyrics in some of my poetry: Ritchie Valens' "Donna," written by Richard Valenzuela (Del-Fi Records, 1958); Rosie and the Originals' "Angel Baby," written by Rosie Méndez-Hamlin (Highland Records, 1960); James and Bobby Purify's "I'm Your Puppet," written by Dewey Lindon "Spooner" Oldham and Dan Penn (Bell Records, 1966); The Buggles' "Video Killed the Radio Star," written by Geoff Downes, Trevor Horn, and Bruce Woolley (Island Records, 1979); the Ramones' "Sheena is a Punk Rocker," written by Joey Ramone (Sire Records, 1977); and X's "Los Angeles," written by John Doe and Exene Cervenka (Slash Records, 1980). Gracias for the lyrics.

Gracias to Dr. Angela Davis for her audio lecture (parts one and two) presented at The Geffen Contemporary at MOCA (The Museum of Contemporary Art). This was The Tornberg Lecture Series for WACK! Art and the Feminist Revolution (June 10, 2007).

A special gracias for José Ramírez for his collaboration with my poems. For this commissioned piece, *ELA*, he captured the energy in creating this beautiful painting for my cover image. I am grateful for all his work.

# Contents

## Epilogue

*For Mama,*

*Julia Socorro Hernández Reyes*
*(15 de junio, 1927 – October 25, 1987)*

*In memories, in my poetry*
*you will always exist.*

*You live in my corazón.*

*Con cariño,*
*Your daughter*

*Verónica "Ronnie"*

## Desert Rain:
### blessing the land

Thick clouds pulled over the cielo like a charcoal rebozo
Loud claps pounded as if manos slapped masa together
thundering their message, "I'm coming . . . I'm coming"
and the withering grass like a viejito perked up to see el barullo
Everyone looked up to the gray-white puffs draping the sky
Nopal and hefty maguey stretched upward for fat drops
They waited so long for summer rains to inspire life—again
And the sky opened its boca and awed a desert rain wind
Streams of plump gotas fell on top of the thirsty tierra
splattering the ground, leaving half lunas on the land

Socorro stepped outside of her blue home near the freeway
Let the warm water wet her brown arms by the awning's edge
She inhaled deeply—moist zacate, tierra, driveway
      "Mmm, Zacatecas. El valle de mi corazón,
        Xochitl. Allá en el pueblito donde yo nací.
        Olía como . . . como ocotillo y tunas."
Xochitl clung to her Amá's pale-blue vestido, smiled
and stared at the big sky while standing on the red porch
Vowed a little sueño to herself and kept it tucked inside
She proclaimed proudly in her six-year-old voice
      "Mmm, Zacatecas, Mami, Zacatecas."
Socorro laughed and with her moist fingers she anointed
herself then her daughter with midday desert rain in the city

The agua took her back to her childhood in México
rain that blessed her alma como copal shrouding her skin
She inhaled the desert aroma over concrete, nopales,
and limones beneath splintered street telephone wires
Socorro breathed in once and inhaled México in East L.A.

# Green Helicopters

the apple-orchard helicopter buzzed buzzed around
    piercing the light-blue sky
    shaking loose brown particles     toxins
    choking the air   the people
    like in a migrant field

✳

at noon the air thickened the sun sliced it
the unripe apple flew across the long rows
it spies green every hour on the brown people
spiraling the streets of sydney, humphreys
tracking their cluttered grounds, their space

✳

the crisp helicopter pulled the blue-tinted cellophane
    suffocating the poor people
    draining the air of oxygen    life
    spraying noise pollution
    like in an infested orchard field

✳

and the canela-tinted borracha slurred
"i'll save your spot" to the oil stain street
the cobalt car sped to the liquor corner
and she stood waiting in    the spot
a forty-five-year-old guarding an oil blotch
    one hand on her blue waist

one hand tilting a bottle
the sun's light sparkled a green glow
and the helicopter hovered for a bit
it swaggered like the drunken lady
    believing she was a parked car
    believing her cerveza was life
and la borracha stared at the green porch
sipped the beer waiting for the cobalt car
a crooked grin splotched her lined mouth
    inside she was silent
    inside she was polluted
and she stared inside herself at night
the green helicopter sliced her thoughts

*years ago she was a schoolteacher*
*taught elementary down at brannick*
*the children loved her called her Mrs.*
*"teacher, teacher, brianislookingatme."*
*she'd smiled with a squint, "huh, mija."*
*and that was all she needed to do*

the apple-orchard helicopter cut the sky
    piercing the souls wandering
    tainting their lives green every    day
    watching the people with a scope
    like criminals in prison

# Marimacha

She strutted down Whittier Boulevard
checking out the rucas on the calle
A bien suave Xicana butch dyke
Hair slicked back with Tres Flores
glistening against her earth tone skin
Cut off khakis right at the knees
smooth crease down the pant legs
Starched-white camisa over an undershirt
    "Fruit of the Looms"
A true homeboy's brand bought at J.C. Penny

Learned how to planchar as a little chamaca
    ironing papi's shirts, pantalones cada madrugada
    ironing her hermanito's school clothes cada día
      No time for studying    No time to be a kid
Learned how to planchar just like her Amá

And when Carmen ran across Fetterly Avenue
amidst the drowning yellow to the stoplight
She placed her palm on her black-lettered belt
and jogged as if the pinche cops were chasing her
      Homebred in East L.A.
Carmen walked like she owned the calles
This barrio was hers   Arizona Maravilla
Carmen strutted down Whittier Boulevard
As she headed towards the Golden Gate Theater
she savored Garfield High School memories
where she used to neck and make out with Josefina
in the back rows hidden by the darkness
A white beam streamed over them like a río
splashing a Pedro Infante movie on the screen

Mmm, Josefina, her main ruca. Era mujer, all mujer.
Firme. Nice smooth curves. Strong hips to cradle
Carmen's body, her tattered soul back into her whole
self. Pressing lips, bodies together. Savoring chocolate
nipples excited her.

"yeah, ese, if i had a penis, a real one, not one of
those pinche plastic shits, i'd move it in, out, make
her beg, ese, for more, i know how to please a mujer,
keep my mija satisfied."

And she rubbed her panza remembering high school days
where she used to make out with Josefina
where no vato o ruca would mess with her
cause they knew she kicked ass like any decent vato

On the streets, Carmen earned the reputation of a peleonera
When she was little, everybody knew que era
"Marimacha"
Porque when Carmen fought, peleó como una pinche loca
con fists, crow bars, patadas y más
And the vata always won the pleitos
Nunca lloró    Nunca gritó
Solamente grunted y cussed out every vato
"Fuck you, puto!    ¡Chúpame, ese!"
On the calles, Carmen earned the respect of a true vato
A homegirl always down for her barrio
And Carmen was damn proud of her reputation
as she strutted down Whittier Boulevard in East L.A.
remembering "La Vida Loca" marimacha style
Y Que!

# Chopper! Chopper!

A yellow stream of light entered the cracked cortinas waking Xochitl up
Outside her window behind her bunk bed she could hear the Saturday morning ritual
"Pop, pop, pop" breaking open the silence like a hand slapping, punching the air
Bullets flying by to round red targets up on the hill in the cops' practice firing range
getting ready to shoot one of the prisoners from Biscailuz Center or Sybil Brand
anyone who escaped the metal confines of civilized justice that peered down on them

Minutes fluttered by like a chuparrosa as she watched Saturday morning cartoons
ate her huevo con chorizo breakfast laughing with mouthfuls at Scooby-Doo
then dressed her little self, soft as an empanada, in blue shorts, t-shirt and her favorite
tennies bought at Zody's to go outside and play with anyone standing on the calle

First she sprinted through the yellow cocina, jumped the little step to the backdoor
She stood at the backdoor for a moment, breathed in dust through the screen door
then announced in chopped English, "Mama, we're going up to the mountain?"
like usual her Amá was lavando ropa sucia or cleaning something in the cuartito
and Socorro smiled at her daughter and scolded her, "No te ensucies, Xochitl."
"Yeah, mama." And little Xochitl ran after her eight-year-old amigos
The same ones who all went to Hammel Street School with three tiers
like an excavation plot she once saw at La Brea Tar Pits on a field trip day

All the curly head, straight-laced chamacos up on Sydney ran up the calle
Xochitl, Pelón, Pepe, Zombie, Ruben and Richard scampered up the loma
And they scattered to Blanchard Avenue then climbed the rickety steps
Left over remnants of a home that once nestled itself on the edge of the hill
Now only the tattered cement base existed as the marker in its memory
They scurried up like mountain lion cubs heading back home to the cave
Just like the one they could see from the bottom of the hollow riverbed
Then headed to the top of the montaña to see lions, headed to Rabbitland or Frogland

They jumped over the fence, landed on the solid dirt dusted with bottles, paper
Trailed up the montaña in search of conejos and spying on prisoners at the top
Pelón led the way trekking over dry bush and the mini-boulders they had to climb
And Xochitl carried the cola of the line of brown chamaquillos hiking up
Off to the side the dry weed crackled, hollow branches like splintered huesos cracked
Someone hushed the group and waited in silence for another sign of life nearby
A loud crunch snapped open like a lion's roar and all of them froze for one second
Then a unison cry for help they all pointed to the noise and yelled with all their fuerza
"Chopper! Chopper! Run! The migra is after us. Run! Chopper! Chopper!"
Inside Xochitl felt the air suck out of her as if the sky was a blue fifties vacuum
Instincts grabbed her feet, her piernas and she ran like an immigrant dodging the border
patrol crossing over el Río Bravo heading to El Paso, Las Cruces, Phoenix, San Diego
Little feet darted, scurried down the loma away from the big dog that was chasing them
The chavalos hit the ground like Go Speed Racer, Zombie was like a Tarahumara runner
and Xochitl was the last in line as she skidded over rocks with her super duper tennies
Each mumbling "Chopper, Chopper" a chant to free themselves from the ragged perro
In a split second they made it to the fence and hopped over it onto the old plot
and screamed "Safe!" then laughed like a payaso was tickling their tummies

On summer nights they played barefooted on the fluffy-green zacate
A sheath of coolness kept them on their toes running around
They jumped off skyscrapers like Superman flying across the sky
They dove off diving pool boards into the pool of fresh cut grass
Off they go from the edge of the red porch onto the square lawn
They played Freeze Tag, Hide 'n' Seek, Ring around the Rosies, Mother, May I?
And once they got bored they took off down the calle towards Folsom
Running in bunches, throwing an orange Nerf football and playing dog pile

Xochitl looked up, pointed to the thick chapapote cielo sparsely speckled with white dots
and yelled with all her might, "Chopper! Chopper!" and they all turned around, stared up
They saw a helicopter flying, a dirty bird, a flying rat, from the green sheriff's station
And with its big flashlight it aimed the white bulb to the blue, yellow homes, the street
From a bullhorn a thick voice sprayed words into the black sky, "We know where you are.
This is the police. We know where you are. This is the police."
And they—Zombie, Pelón and Pepe—screamed to the sky in high pitches
"We're here! Over here! We're over here!" and they all ran to the white light
in tired chanclas, worn tennies, Xochitl and her little crew ran to the spotlight
They aimed for the circle of whiteness piercing the black-paved ground
They jumped to the center to stay in it for a moment, long enough to scream
"We're here! We're here! Over here! Look at us we're here! H-e-r-e!"
But the flashlight kept on moving to different sections of the dark road
and the chamacos ran every which way they could to land in the white light
To stand long enough in the brightness like movie stars spotlighted in their night
And they screamed running after the big flashlight splattering white light everywhere

The cops announced to the convict, "We know where you are. We know . . . "
And Xochitl ran out of breath chasing the big white light piercing the darkness
She stopped and stared up at the helicopter slicing the chapapote sky for a moment
It was almost as if it were stuck like the mammoths, the saber-toothed tiger, the Chumash
woman whose bones remained deep underground until the archaeologists came
The people screamed and wailed to be set free from the tar that pulled them down
that swallowed them little by little as they struggled to get out from the bottom
Still the thick goo engulfed them whole suffocating their skin, filling their mouths
Xochitl's brown eyes stared at the chopper swirling in East L.A.'s summer sky
But the helicopter broke free, pulled back its white light and flew away to the hill

And they all stopped panting while looking at *it* fly back to the other side
Xochitl smiled at her friends and tagged Pelón on the shoulder, "You're it!"
They all ran again hiding in yards, behind rusted cars playing the night away . . .

18

# Trockas

Each angel city morning, golden or charcoal painted sky
clusters of them, like tender nopales, break the day open
They travel winding city-smog roads heading to the spot
They travel in threes or fours and sometimes solitary
They so desperately want to blend in with the people
The local born Mexicans who straddle the river, the city
But they look like pesetas, not pennies tossed out

The Mexican born men cross the streets becoming one heap
The Mexican born men's hair shines with brilliantine
The aroma of tiny flores glides behind their trail
But the signs give them away to the people, the cops
Some of them wear rugged jeans
        the usual: Wranglers, Lees, Levi's
Some of them wear polyester pants
        the usual: green, blue, gray
Some of them wear hats
        the usual: vaquero, trucker, baseball
Some, the others wrapped in ponchos from pueblitos
Most items bought at Tres Hermanos, K-Mart stores
trimming the streets on Whittier Boulevard or Brooklyn

In their hands, they carry scrunched brown paper bags
mirroring their lives—creased linings on their bodies
Others swing plastic market bags along their sides
a reflection of their cultura, their lives back home
burritos de arroz y frijol wrapped in aluminum foil
leftover tacos of carnitas carefully sealed in wax paper
Someone—a wife, a novia, a tía, a compa's jefa

Someone woke up before the sun rose to greet her
Someone gently and carefully fixed his afternoon meal
They walk distances from dos bloques to half a mile
All of them head to a corner, the "unofficial" location
  Each looking for the same thing
  Each hoping today is a good day
   "¿Hay trabajo aquí?"


On the esquina of Pomona and Atlantic Boulevard
The young woman in a Mexican flowered blouse
sees them piled like raw-splintered boards leaning
  waiting at the gum-layered corner
  waiting for work to come call them
Older men, young guys press up against the wall
Some are hombres who could be her abuelo
stubbly gray old men wearing cowboy hats
Others young enough to be her little hermano
fresh clean faces still unscathed by a razor
Some of them took a leap of faith in mid age
Each one trailing the street waiting for work
Each one eyeing people glancing at them
Each one eyeing trockas slowing to a halt


And when the man in la trocka rolls up
it is a game of economics the men must play
The Mexicanos suddenly perk up into a line
and the truck man eyes each one like a hawk
He asks the question, the type of work he needs
  "¿Hay alguien que sabe trabajar en techo?"

The Mexican men step out announcing skills
        some of them say their work history
        some of them say "i'm a fast learner"
        some of them say whatever necessary
The trocka man picks his three workers
Each one waits with hearts stomping
Each one waits hoping it is me chosen
Each one waits needing the money
They negotiate their price like salesmen
settle their deal with a handshake, a nod

They jump up over the side rail as if it's a fence
crossing over a desert, a river, a wall
In the truck's bed, they sit on the edges
        finding an empty spot
        finding a place to stand
        making his own spot
Someone, a señor, is perched by the window
like an águila with a serpent in its beak
They have returned to their ancestor's tierra
The ones left behind will wait on the corner
and the trocka drives off down the street
as if it is spitting gravel at the Mexicans

In the dark, they all travel back home again
And the half moon resembles their lives here
They will sleep in fits east of the city landscape
under the gaze of two águilas watching them
In the madrugada, they will break the day open

# Torcidaness: Tortillas and me

You know, a homemade tortilla de maíz when you see it
All crooked, lopsided and torcida like queer Silver Lake
Ya sabes, que it ain't round and curved like una pelota
Ya sabes, que it ain't no flying saucer like at Roswell
Tú sabes, homegirl, esta pura chueca like the owner
                              Me

Back when I was a little chamaca o mocosa
A kid, a rowdy one, from the barrios of East L.A.
I knew I was a little torcida, just a little
a little off to the side on the edge, tú sabes
Not straight, you know what I mean
I had it in me to be a little torcida and I loved it!
Tú sabes, homes, how it is in—el barrio

Back then on Sydney Drive and Floral in Belvedere District
Oscar's store at the esquina near the alley was the place to be
We'd hang out and play:  Centipede  Asteroids  Pac Man
or Ms. Pac Man (Oh yeah, like she really needed a man)
and even Galaga. . . . Can you hear it? Tu, tu, tu . . . (very Mexican ¿que no?)
Tu, tu, tu (Can you hear Eydie Gormé? Oh, how so East L.A.) Tu, tu, tu . . .
Coming at you . . . faster faster—Oh shit. Blast! You're dead.

No more pinball shit for us   that was 1970-something mierda
We were the generation of Atari—the beginning of digital games
We created the "Simon Says" electronic style ¡Y Qué!
We played games like "Merlin" that used six double-A batteries
and only lasted, if you were lucky, maybe one week or two

In fact: this was the Pre-Gummy Bear era, Pre-Digital world, baby
This was clean-white Vans with no shoelaces and no socks required
Or checkered black and white Vans slip-ons with graffiti on plastic sides
Polo shirts with the little alligator growling at anyone who stares

This was the time of long-haired guys wearing thermal shirts under
black short-sleeved shirts that blared, "Iron who?" on the front
And raised a finger in angst yelling, "Iron Fuckin' Maiden"

This was Siouxsie and the Banshees' era with deep black mascara
The gothic singer who hung out with Robert Smith and Morrissey
The Smiths who dominated airwaves of Mexican Impala cars
The time of the original Pretenders "Back on the Chain Gang"
Chrissie Hynde kicking it with Cyndi Lauper's waffle-side haircut
All of them to be out-dressed, outshined by the only    Boy George
The original drag queen, transvestite loved by straight people

This was just hanging and spying, *Fast Times at Ridgemont High*
Or trying to get a bootleg copy of *The Decline of Western Civilization*
Just to see a few brown Mexican faces: Alice Bag, Robert López
slamming, screaming in the static Penelope Spheeris's film

Or desperately begging a friend to get a pirated copy of the banned
yet acclaimed film. . . . Yes, you heard right, acclaimed film:
　　　*The Rocky Horror Picture Show*
Love that Tim Curry in tight corset, fishnet stockings, drag queen all the way
Yep, this is how I knew these were the blossoming times of my torcidaness

The beginning of something really queer was   happening here
Cause all I wanted to do was hang out at Retail Slut dressed in black

like all the other queers on Melrose Avenue near Highland
Oh, so close to West Hollywood yet so far away from East L.A.
And be my little self amongst all the gay-white-boys who strolled
Christopher Street with their little tight white shorts Wham! style

So this is what we did to get to the suave '80s retail joint
Call it dedication by three "desperate" Mexican Americans
Trying to find a spot in this crazy place gringos populated
We'd hop the 30 to la Primera and Broadway near the State Building
Crossed the big O' four-lane calle and wait for the 10 to cruise on by
Hop that sucker and take a whirlwind of a RTD ride for an hour
Just to get to, yes, Hollywood—the one and only Tinsel Town
Get to our main attraction, sightsee, window shop just like the gringos
Oh, sure sometimes we had a mission to buy something like purple Docs
Or something more chingón to be like esa, Drew, in blue Monkey boots
Yeah, when we had a mission, we stood there all sábado afternoon
roaming gringo Hollywood on Melrose and blended in with crowd
More like we blended in with the brown custodian workers or cooks


But hey, this is the eighties and we're listening to Elvis Costello
Banging our heads on walls following Billy Zoom into X land
"Long live Punk!" it's a way of life not just a style of music
Just gotta love that Exene screaming "Los Angeles!" over and over
The banging of drums, the screeching of guitars, the bass pounding
Oh yeah, I can hear it now all in my head "She had to leave. . . ."
Kinda reminds me of Joey Ramone bobbing his shiny black hair
Shouting, not singing you know, "Sheena is . . . a punk rocker . . ."

Yeah, I grew up in the era of MTV the first radio-music videos ever
Because after all "Video killed the radio star / Video killed the radio star"
Yep, if you grew up in East L.A., you watched MV3 on Channel 13
Public videos for one hour at four or five in the evening after school
     No more of that "After School Special" shit
     We were eighties kids all the way
Back then we ate it up like it was enchiladas rojas: hot and good chisme
gossiped about the new video, Richard Blade at every lunch period
Yep, this was the eighties and I was learning my crookedness

✳

Hey so listen up: so there I was strolling down the calle to the tienda
You know how it is at thirteen, my mama sent me for un mandado
So I hopped inside to grab some paquete de tortillas I was sent for
Pulled the first paquete of Guerrero o Princesa on top of the stack
Paid the original Oscar's who the store is named after for
And took off like a dirty shirt just like *Pretty in Pink*
Strolled back up the calle to bring back these tortillas de maíz

And then it happened:   when I wasn't even doing nothing
There I was pretending to be Superman so I could get Lois
Twirling, flying with my brown arms stretched out up down up
And then out of nowhere the pinche tortillas started to fly
There the chingaderas went flying like Space Invaders
Little round tortillas, mmm tortillas, raining everywhere
They landed on graffiti cement, on the oil-stained pavement
On leftover beer bottles near greasy tires of used carros

I stopped in mid-flight watching everything go and I freaked out
My mama was gonna whip my little brown nalga with the cinto
The Mexican kind with the metal tip she always threatened me with
Goddamn, I could feel the hot whips piercing my eighth grade piernas
I ran and picked up all those precious tortillas and stuffed them inside
Chingado, I turned the pinche bag and it had a clean rip on its side
Went back to ese, Oscar, and showed him: See—proof, I needed a new one
The viejo let me go with a new bag, and I clutched it to my flat chest
and I ran up Sydney Drive's loma like the pinche migra was after me


Hey, so that's my story of tortillas and me
I say a pretty good one, ¿que no?
The beginning of my torcida days to come
And now pues, ya sabes
Soy la mera mera marimacha ¡Y Qué!

# Mariachi Plaza 1990

## I. Los Trabajadores

Red graffiti, black placazos splash the concrete riverbed
L.A. water trickles down the raw edge of el Boyle Heights
In the madrugada, the scrawny esquina bursts with gente
A tiny-yellow donut shop sits on Boyle and First Street
Stocky men, mujeres maduras step outside the tienda
with steaming café, *La Opinión* and a bolsa de donas
They wait fifteen-twenty minutes on a concrete island
Sometimes señoritas step on warm pink chicle
leaving stretched gum with tennies' print on the sidewalk
Sometimes señores' leathered botas tramp on aceite stains
leaving a half print of themselves on the sidewalk
Old jalopies parked—someone's Impala, dented Toyota
and the workers dash off to el centro on bus number 30 or 31.

The passengers cram wrinkled billetes into a new fare box
and everyone is stuffed inside the tagged buses like green dolares
They travel over la Primera's puente to el Centro, el otro lado
Pass Little Tokyo, the Far East restaurant and the blue police station
Someone, a newcomer, always pulls the bell one too many times
Some pile out of the piloncillo bus on First and Broadway
Upon exiting "Gracias" and saludos drape the air for the RTD driver
Blue-gray skyscrapers tower over them like the güero manager
And on Bunker Hill, they clean offices, they mop restrooms
      Old men, tatas at home, clean gringo law offices
      Old señoras, abuelas at home, sweep government buildings
In the Jewelry District, young women sew in high rises
In the Garment District, clothing for Hollywood lights
      hundred dollar dress shirts, three-hundred vestidos

In all sweatshops, they breathe thread, breathe steam
into their raw pulmones that will clog later on in life.

And when the evening comes shrouding the city
a wrinkled-blue latex twilight wraps the sun people
The workers, someone's papi, mami, rush the calles
heading east over el puente into el Boyle, their home.

## II. La Plaza de la Raza

Every evening the face of First and Boyle reawakens
as streams of brown faces walk the calles' capillaries
Mexican men dressed in black mariachi suits seep
through the bloody arteries that breathe life into L.A.

Los musicantes as if Villistas emerge on the esquina
Like notitas, the men line up with their instruments:
       el violín, la guitarra, the trumpet
       and el guitarrón float in the air
On the side of pant leggings, silver or gold trinkets
trail along the trim just like the men waited all noche
long with brown coyotes ready to cross el Río Bravo.

Music scales hum a sweet tune in the smoggy air
Norteñas, rancheras swim in each high note
reaching for the dream on the "promised" tierra
They all believed, once, comida—frijoles, arroz
and plentiful jobs surfaced on this side of the border.

At 9:00 Boyle and la Primera glitters with cobalt
rojo and morado sunset tingeing the brown sky
The hues shrouded in Hidalgo's Grito de Dolores
The tired sol settles to sleep behind blue-gray edificios.

And in the onyx noche, gray sueños wail to come true
like the colorful evenings when trockas arrive for musicians
And the brazen man picks and chooses mariachis for a fiesta
mirroring the way a butcher slices N.Y. steaks for customers
Always choosing the best musicantes like Grade A meat.

## III. The Golden Sueño

In East L.A.—el Boyle, City Terrace, Belvedere
on the other side of the puente streaming over el río
stale crumbs are tossed to the people to feed their families
Mariachi Plaza breathes life into the Mexican streets
and en la noche mariachis sing a ranchera for the worker.

# El Violinista

When the sun begins to fall asleep, the moon blinks her eyes once, twice
and the sky shades the horizon turquoise into deep blue with green tinges
And the sol bleeds a ripe granada bursting open on the earth's canvas
El señor ambles to the musty recámara, then rummages in his locked closet
pulls out a weathered case he's had for sixty-some-odd years of his life
And he, rickety like a wooden cross in Zacatecas, readies himself to play: el violín
An evening ritual he performs every evening living in his small home

Señor Jaramillo sits on the edge of the bed staring out the recámara's ventana
dreaming of boyhood days bathed in desert air in el Valle de Valparaíso
He sees his long lonely treks to Fresnillo, the nearest pueblo, and back home
spending frost-desert nights near manteles of ocotillo, chaparral y nopal
(a roughly woven table cloth covers the dark brown earth he nestles on)

His mind flips through images of his youth and focuses on a few snapshots:
  a cafecito man, really un joven, working en el rancho branding vaca
  playing el violín in the cobblestone zócalo como siempre enticing
  the young mujeres
Each pluck of the taut string, each arch of the bow, each quarter note
lassoed the beautiful mujeres to speak to him, to flatter him: el violinista
Then his dark brown eyes glint and his wrinkles like mapas tell stories
Jaramillo smiles, laughs a little remembering those youthful days en el Valle

Gently, he pulls out his scuffed violin case and places it like a host
in the maroon mouth of el león roaring, a print on a San Martín blanket
Years ago, 1938, he bargained with a viejito, un antiguo de esos tiempos,
in the windblown desert of his pueblito, shrouded in a sheath of sand
The old man twirled un cuento for young ears, canela red from el sol
"Bueno dicen que un chaparro played for Zapata's bigote negro. Lo dicen."
But it was only a chiste, a revolution cuento somebody shared with him once

He opens the black case, admires the artwork of fine-tuned hollow wood
A soft bed of white resin glistens near the bridge holding the four strings
With an old kerchief, Señor Jaramillo polishes the grain lengthwise to prepare it
then cradles the slender neck in his calloused, scarred, factory-worker hand
His arthritic fingers loom over the black pegs then he harmonizes the squeals
After all these años, it still sings beautiful swirling zapateando melodies
Jaramillo lays a neatly folded pañuelo with a sewn ♪ letter on his shoulder
Carefully, he positions el violín under his wrinkled chin, arches his arms and plays:
norteñas, rancheras, some boleros and "Happy Birthday" songs for his kids

At eighty-four or six, he still has the round-smooth muscle in his right arm
He claims he ate a special "desert conejo" and it planted itself—there
He always tells this tale to all the niños before the big story of crossing over:
        "Cuando yo era niño trabajé mucho.
        Crucé este pueblo, donde nací, hasta
        el otro. No había nadie caminando.
        Nomás estaba la luna y yo."
The story grows while he sits on the blue sofa sharing his life in the old country
He weaves a cuento of Villistas, gente indígena, peyotes and puros ladrones
He was in el Valle crossing from one pueblo to the next back in the mid '20s
Stayed the night under the dark-blue sarape sky, glittering with tiny-white luces
Cooked a brown rabbit for cena over a crackling fire fat juices sizzling on the flame
Once he ate it, the buena suerte energy got stuck there—the center of his right arm
He flexed his brazo, patted his muscle, a reminder of his juventud back en la sierra

By the blue curtain, dust particles dance in the evening air and leave the day's stage
In the twilight hours, he sits on the same spot on the chenille twin bed that he kept
With his wife, they bought it on venta, a bunk bed from Wenger's on Whittier
Most of his eight children slept on it, made good use of his Vernon factory pay

Jaramillo squirms a bit to get comfortable near the peeling ventana looking out
Then he stretches his fingers, each one a brown-tethered knot from hard work
Sangre, like agua santa, cures the stiffness away bringing back youth to him

Slowly, he begins to play his violin and the music streams from a young man
The notas float out the screen mesh over the zacate through the umbrella tree
into the barrio of Sydney Drive, leaving a trail of music climbing the homes
Neighbors up, down the street hear him playing for an hour around 7 p.m.
His melody caresses the purple-blue cielo and falls in love with México again
Señor Avalos, a vecino, sits on his stucco porch, sipping cerveza and he dreams
Jaramillo closes his murky eyes, feels la música and this viejito's body vanishes
He is a young caballero tocando violín for his compadres drinking tequila reposado
He is the young caballero who fell in love one Valparaíso summer cobalt evening

One yellow-moon noche, young Jaramillo saw her with her friends, primas strolling
His eyes followed her, he recalled she was just a girl when he saw her in a tiendita
Her clothing seemed to be an old bolsa de harina, a washed out flowered dress
She was buying *cal*, lime powder for tortillas de maíz, for her Abuela Concepión
Full of buck, he leaned into the tina, grabbed a handful and draped her hands in white
      "Si te quedas aquí en este pueblo toda
         tu vida, nomás vas a hacer tortillas."
He smiled, proudly announced to her he would marry her and take her to el otro lado
He said she would not spend her youth making tortillas for a husband in this town

Now, a grown woman walking en el zócalo, he was awed by her presence again
Jaramillo in a finely pressed shirt, black shined shoes and smelling of Tres Flores
abruptly stood up and took a shot of tequila, then gallantly strode up to her
"Te acuerdas de mi." He smiled, she smiled, No, and he smiled, again

With canciones and pláticas de hombre y mujer, he won her corazón
La luna llena's yellow sash of light bound them that summer evening

✳

In the crook of the loma's bend between Eastern and Floral, el violín sings
For Jaramillo in his recámara, music soothes his corazón and warms his alma
Vivid images always flood him: he relives his youth and remembers his wife
Forty years of marriage on the other side of el Río Bravo as he promised her
and when he puts his violín away to rest, he tucks his memories away for the night
The blue-black sky shimmers tiny luminarias and the moon soothes him to sleep

# The Nopal Garden

## I. The Past

The yarda was once filled with yonke:
white bolsas draped the chaparral
dry branches clutched white sheets
The small lot—thin as a drug addict

The sun ate forgotten objects:
jaundiced bottles scatter the area
clear botellas nicked, half-buried bodies
all plants, scraps broken in murky sand

And in this dead lot of junk on Humphreys
Marijuana, like the calle Floral, blossomed

## II. *El jardín de nopalitos*

Seven years shed away all the cascabeles
A wrought iron fence wraps around the plot
as if a molten-black tower peers over cacti
No one steps on the dirt lot by the bus stop
Rows like onion fields fill the corner space

Before the planting of mota in dark spots
Before the paper lunch bags hidden away
a marigold home lived on this corner

Chavela, la señora Isabel from Michoacán
They say she was una de esas, a malflora
A lovely woman who never married
La Señora Chavela who taught violín

She'd play arpeggios singing to el cielo
Sometimes she played "El Cascabel" for her
Her best "friend" who never made it across
In the desert she vanished amongst nopales
Once Chavela's ahijada came to take care of her
La Señora said "No" and planted seeds in her jardín
Las flores blossomed orange, tinges of rojo, yellow
They say this was her amiga's perfect flor
La caléndula for los espíritus del otro lado
and around the red porch stood one nopal
Crimson prickly pears pierced the sky's rebozo
When Chavela left la ciudad de los ángeles
the old ones say she flew back to Michoacán
like a chuparrosa singing, returning home

## III. The Present

Seven years drifted away in the small lot
And in the air, violins of el cascabel sing
Rows of nopalitos frame the tierra lot
Each desert plant protecting the spirits
The way she protected her red-orange home
The way her lover, Pati, protected Chavela
A lone nopal amongst a beautiful marigold

# El Bus

Hey, you know, I speak in bus routes
I can tell you any pinche bus number
you need to know to get you around
Take the 18 down Whittier Boulevard
to check out the East L.A. scenery
    El CHOC—a chingón thrift store
    Out of the Closet—for all the jotos y dykes
    Porky's—the Mexican restaurant for your tummy
    and all the vendors from young to old on the sidewalk
        Hay cassettes para everyone
        Fresh verduras con chile y sal

And you know, I even know
the Montebello system, too
Take the number 10 to ELAC near Pomona
It zooms down Atlantic Boulevard
quicker than any MTA bus
a.k.a. Muggers Thieves Association
Or take the 40 down Beverly
It blends right into Third Street
Fly by the East L.A. Library and el parque de los patos
and swing on by Guadalupe Church, rosas and Calvary

Yes, my friends, I speak in bus routes
I'm the ruca who can tell you
how to get from here—to there
in several different bus number lines
Take the 256 on Eastern Avenue to Pasadena
It cuts through El Sereno, Highland Park
picking up all the señoras to clean the gringos' casas

Drops them off on the corner to walk up a loma
in South Pasadena then heads straight into Old Town

You got it, esa or ese, I know the system
It's in my blood to travel the calles via el bus
I know its ins and outs like my own brown mano
who hands over the last of my little cambio
I even know the fregado drivers a.k.a. los operators
who'd run you over just for fun
who make you run to get the bus
who slam the puerta on your face, arm
Yes, I know the good, the bad, and the pinche ugly
I know all the locos y locas who drive
        El bus

Yes, people, I speak in bus routes
Take the 68 to hop on over to the Chicano mall
a.k.a. the Montebello Town Center
Travel down Brooklyn Avenue, now César Chávez
Check out the colorful talavera building by Gage
Sightsee the colorful Mexican calle that crosses over
the big frontera into crispy-clean Monterey Park
then skids right into Montebello near the freeway
Hey, and those young people come dressed
in their finest Sunday clothes working the runways
a.k.a. they stroll the second floor walkways

I can tell you to take the 30, originally the 26
to skate the dips and turns of First Street
pass la mera mera tienda—La Primera

You know, the place with the 1970's Aztec warriors
Stay on the 31 and check out the Chinese Cemetery
then land right smack in Atlantic Square

Yes, my friends, I speak in bus routes
I know the ways of the calles on el bus
I can tell you any pinche bus number
you need to know to get you around
Yes, my people, I speak in bus routes

# Recycling: 1976

Prologue:

*When I was a little girl, a seven-year-old one, we collected cans—they all still had the pull-out tab that left a red mark in your dedo, like a little dent, the kind that cut clean into tender finger tips—we, my hermanos and I, collected old coors or budweiser botes, tab, aspen soda cans, any cans really—cans from metal trash cans, from dingy gutters, from dirt-layered sidewalks, from wherever someone left a can on the ground, on the zacate, tossed by the lake at Lincoln Park, half buried in the sandbox just like the statue of liberty in* planet of the apes . . .

*When I was a niña back in the mid seventies, collecting cans was a game we played with Apá—it was an adventure to hang out with him, diggin' into trashcans, draining syrupy soda, getting as many cans as we can hold in our small brazos, so we can win against one another—I'd grab a whole bunch with all my fuerza so I can win against my sister or chamaco brother or even better to beat Apá by a million botes—it was what we did after a whole day spent at the beach . . .*

*This was how we spent our summer evenings at Long Beach.*

## I. Recycling estilo Mexicano

The gordito sun dipped below the red-black Queen Mary horizon
Off to the ocean's center behind the breakers, the little palm trees waved
The tall-thin buildings in pastel shades hid the city's oil refineries
On the way to the beach, we'd see old dinosaurs bobbing their heads
metal tongues like needles drilling deep into wet tierra for black sangre
I'd learned at La Brea that dinosaurs' bones became fossil fuel
Big mammoths trapped in gooey tar pits that sucked them slowly down
"Look, ese, dinosaurs!" I'd smack my brother or sister on the arm
We stared, eyes pinned, to witness the bones of woolly mammoth

At the end of the day, we'd follow Apá to search for botes
        our dark brown skins caked with white linings of sea salt
        our hair matted with sand just like our dry swimsuits
Our beach clothes bought at zody's or gemco's stores or la Primera
We scurried along the beach's parking lot searching for our treasure
And peered inside botes de basura for pepsi, rc, coke, or michelob cans
We'd grab two or three, run and find Papa standing by the dumpster
give 'em our findings like gold coins, our tesoro, then scamper off
        "Apá, aquí esta uno and here's another one."
        "Ronnie, agárrame ese bote que está allá. ¡Córrele!"
And I'd take off like the bionic woman running super duper fuerte
trying to get as many cans to win, the prize a seat by the window
And if I won, I rolled the ventana down and stuck my tongue out to dry
We'd pile and pile botes in two or three plastic bags—some smashed some not
Then we'd drive back to East L.A. on the 7 Freeway to our blue home

All of the botes dumped into the fat aluminum can near the Aztec mural
The crooked boca swallowing each one to change like straw into money
Collecting cans was for the little extra-dinero my dad could make
It was for the collection to be added to the big-dented trashcan outside
The one where my dad placed his "new" botes after they were smashed
After the hill of cans grew, my dad sat down on the zacate—legs sprawled
He'd struggle to kneel down to sit with his rickety rodillas, wobbly like jello
Severe arthritis from slaughterhouse work walking in knee high warm cow's
blood then stepping into freezers where fresh carcasses waited to be sliced
Reumas locked his old knees and gave him stiff joints that panged

On a Friday evening, cobalt splashed the sky; after the mowing of the lawn
he'd plop himself down near the green tool shed and hammer away
Carefully, taking each can, standing it into an assembly line, and whacking it
Each bote a nail smashed into the ground becoming only a shiny head

With each fregazo, it got tossed into the big can that looked like Oscar the Grouch's home
Then off he'd go on a sábado morning after breakfast—frijoles, huevo y papas
we'd see him get in the station wagon and go to a recycling center to get cash

When he'd come home in the grumpy wagon, we knew there was dinero for us
We'd go to la Primera or Atlantic Square to j.c. penny's to buy stuff with Amá
to buy school clothes, the usual: socks, chonis, pants, shirts, and school supplies
And with the little leftover, my Amá strolled down the first floor of newberry's
to buy rolls of yarn, all sparkly, for knitting to make doilies, baby shoes, a blanket
and sometimes, if we'd went to the mercado, she'd buy day-old van de kamp's pastries
from la Central; the dinero from the botes was to buy the *little extra things*

## II. Summertime Reflections

Back when I was a kid, recycling was not for saving the environment from toxic pollutants—
when I was a kid, collecting cans was for the extra money that my Apá's pension and our social
security checks did not cover for us—recycling was somewhat for economic survival for a
family of five living on limited income, maybe it was fourteen or fifteen thousand a year but it
was probably less than that—recycling was a way so that we'd never know we were *poor*—when
I was a little one, collecting cans was a way to bond a father-daughter relationship into a solid-
respectable one, and it worked.

## Epilogue:

Even now at eighty-seven or nine, my Apá dressed in pressed slacks, crisp dress shirt, polished
zapatos, comes home from church—Guadalupe o Soledad—and he's carrying an empty can he
found somewhere on the calle—and he says "Tírelo en la caja roja," his new recycling bin—now
he fills this plastic container 'til it's full and waits for a vecino, a sober veterana changing her life
or anyone trudging up the loma with a supermarket cart collecting cans from the big blue bins
and they'll call to him "Oiga señor, ¿tienes botes?" or he'll call to them "Tengo más botes atrás."
And he sends 'em to the backyard.

# Los Angeles River—Río Grande:
## brown-speckled mirrors

I. Was it a sueño?

Beneath the old Juárez-El Paso International Puente,
slabs of cement layer the brown banks. They strangle.
And the agua suffocates the drowning gente braving el río.
In sloshes the water releases the screams up to Cihuacoatl.
Along the thick sides of el Río Grande, women, men,
and students from both sides spray red, black placazos.
Politics lace the bordered fortress dividing tierra y familias.

And in the smoggy city of angelitos, officials killed her.
El río de Los Ángeles, a reflection of el Río Bravo,
trails down a 1930's gringo-made route cutting the canela dirt.
Patchwork of yellow chaparral and desert line the brown agua.
DWP sewers empty the city's discharge like piss into the water.
Painted cat faces—yellow, black, stripped, orange—smile openly.
Sewer lips hiss a murky río dumping pulp, botellas and soiled bags.
All of it travels down the water-body curves of la Llorona.
Day and night she screams as if birthing a shopping cart.

They say California was once México living in Aztlán:
The Anasazi, the Ventura people, la Mexica existed here.
On this arid land, this State, there lived many nations.
They were a living part of the living blue seacoast:

> in a dream, seashells were money. half of a mussel was a spoon.
> the acorn source of a stable diet. women crushed them, seeped
> away the toxins, boiled the mush with hot rocks, and made a meal.

The Chumash, Pomo, Modoc people walked on this land.
The red-brown people once co-existed with the dolphin.
Years ago on this terrain, they lived with many Nations:
     And the white man's "legal" papers killed people
     And the white man's government killed families
     And the white man announced, "Terminated!"
On federal papers, the people's nations were slashed.
Red ink ran across the Coastal Band of the Chumash,
across many people as if they did not exist in body, spirit.
They vanished into white ocean mist under a white sun.

    "Was it a dream that the earth lived and breathed
      blue skies so freely?"

Like many ancestors, el río de Nuestra Señora la Reina de Los Ángeles
once roared powerfully with pure life, until *they* came.
Now, it is suffering from disease, a water ailment, the way its compadre,
el Río Grande, suffers in the Chihuahuan desert near ASARCO plant.
Companies, big and small, secrete waste—chemicals, sewage—
And people toss garbage cans, black tires like discarded tribal bands.
Caution signs wobble—illness, ignorance infests the murky water canal
and peligro waits the way a black culebra patiently waits for prey.

And the red-brown children from both sides wade in and out
playing along la frontera that separates familias.

II. Is it a dream?

As I take the #30 bus down to el Centro,
we cross over la Primera Street puente

from Boyle Heights to Broadway Avenue.
I stare out the graffitied window:
sliced slabs of cement cradle the canal,
the L.A. River decapitated from the land.

At the edge of the concrete bordering the water,
a man stands hunched over, bathing his body.
With cold brown agua prickling his skin,
he spreads the polluted grime onto himself.

*In the Zacatecas, Jalisco, Sonora, he left his familia.*
*His daughter waits for him by the puerta.*
*Her mother tells her, "Papi will be back soon."*
*And the heavy sun settles itself beneath Tonantzín.*

"Why is he bathing in a dead río?"

Este hombre could be my tío, mi papá, my brother.
He is my gente, my sangre from México.
Raza that comes across la frontera to survive
like my familia who worked en la pisca
on the outskirts of Denver, where my Apá nació.
El año we do not know—it was never recorded.
They do not exist on paper.

# Cholo Lessons Por Vida

Calling all homeboys, rucas, OGs! Calling all of you to pay attention!
Yes, your life will and can have future meaning in your veterano days
So here it goes; on the way to the airport it slipped out of your sister's boca
So, yeah, Abel was now a chef, a cement worker, a repairman, a workaholic
His former cholo days-gone-vato-loco were gone like illegal fireworks
Now the ex-homeboy lives in "husbandlandia," a pinche far, faraway land
Yes, you heard, his former cholo days now are "father titles" that he lives for
He cooks, cleans, waters the garden, builds things and takes care of the kids
Yep, his cholo days are long gone but they have come in handy as a family man
Can you believe it, carnales and carnalas, the streets were his textbooks?
Chingao, there are so many fregado things he learned from the calles!
Goddamn, who says cholo days can't come in handy?
Who says cholos are wasting their Mexican lives?

Frankly, esa y ese, here are all the things he learned from calle to casa
From his rugged barrio days and out in the calles like un pinche vago
as mi mamá called him as she pulled his orejas, yanking him this way that way
dragging him inside the blue-chuparrosa casa so he could stop being a big O vago
So the vato learned the skills and ways to be, yes, a "family man"

Lesson One:    Remember those days of creasing khaki pants with starch
so that your pantalones couldn't move. Like it was pinche
iron pants from "Ironside." These skills as a cholo gone loco
using extra starch can be used by a family man today. When
your kids are getting ready for school en la mañana. Take out
those Catholic school clothes and crease them, navaja sharp,
like you did in the old days con ganas a matar some crazy
vato from some other territory. Go ahead, ese, iron those
green-white checkered clothes.

Remember to double crease your little vato's pants and white t-shirt so you can feel like your calle knowledge has come into use for you as an adult with chamacos hanging onto your side. Let your kids go to school looking bien suave and smelling like Tres Flores. Brillante is the way to go.

Lesson Two:     Oh, comida. You know, cocinando burritos on the run. Yeah, it was like you knew cooking would come in handy. All those times you ran out the back door to hang out with the vatos from la Lopez. You tossed the tortillas de harina on the black iron comal. Heated up some frijoles with chorizo. Or warmed up bolognie on the llama to wrap up in a burnt tortilla and take off to the calles. Pretending you were some cool vato with burrito in hand cause all the vatos did it. Claiming his jefa cooked him some food to go. These cooking skills have come into play now as daddy of three—two crazy little chamacos like you and one señorita like her Amá.

Get breakfast ready before they go to school. Cook the biggest guajolote for día de thanksgiving to eat for days. As we Mexicans like to call it, the day we munch out while the gringo pilgrims pray we let them live. Chingao what a mistake? We should've known from the stench not to trust them. Puritan, que nada.

Lesson Three:     Smashed jardines. Trampled rosas. Taking care of the yarda. Yeah, remember all those times you were running from the pinche cops and you jumped over fences and ran through neighbors' backyards. Stepped on rose bushes or even fell on mama's rose bushes. Now is the time for pay back, ese. You get up every pinche madrugada just like your Amá and water those plantas like it's a ritual for all the smashing of rosas and breaking backyard sillas when hanging out with rucas. Taking care of the yard so it don't get trampled.

Lesson Four: Graffiti. Writing your placazo on the walls. On the cement sidewalks. Using your cholo penmanship, Old English, to scribble your identity on the paredes of someone's house. Stone wall fences on Sydney and Folsom. Well ese, now you gotta make cement foundations for the County. This ain't no jail time from juvie sent to clean up your mess. Just like that job you had from the Maravilla Projects painting houses. Frankly, ese, this is your day job to make cement floors. Life is not without its irony in it. Ain't it vato loco sent to life to work as cement worker? As you said once "I like to spit on my cement. To see if it's dry yet." S-h-i-t, spit all you want ese. So homes, escaping la chota and jumping fences has definitely come in handy, ¿que no?

Lesson Five: Cruising. Remember those days of cruising down Whittier Boulevard and hooking up with as many rucas as you can because you thought you were irresistible with those deep dimples when you smiled. And strutted down the calle like you were the only one who belonged there. Or you cruised with your homeboys in your aqua-blue bomb with a white top, a.k.a. lowrider, checking out the scene, whistling, catcalling to some ruca from another gang. Just to get your play on some other vato's girlfriend. To get the thrill that you were better

than some other vato. Yeah, remember that you cruised all
night long before the cops came and yanked you out the cars.
Beat your asses. Well, those cruising days are over. Now you
got to work your nalga off to pay off two cars. One for you
and the other for your only daughter. She costs a lot just to keep
her happy. Kind of reminds you of some old times, doesn't it?
But the cops, ese, well they still stop your brown ass. When you
drive down any calle that they think you don't belong in. Just a
reminder that, yes, you were a vato loco, a homeboy from East L.A.
No vale pura madre.

Lesson Six:    Boxers. Back in those youthful days you strutted around the house
in your Fruit of the Loom boxers, a genuine cholo brand, bought at
JC Penny or la Primera store or K-Mart or Zody's where your mama
bought them on sale. And it didn't matter to you cause you still walked
around the cold linoleum barefooted into the living room. Plopped
yourself on the blue couch and watched Saturday morning cartoons.
And some vato, maybe Cuate 1 or Cuate 2 (who knows, we couldn't
tell), would yell, "Abel! Is Abel here?" And you peeked through the
blue curtains, pulled up your boxers like you're straightening your ropa.
And walked out into the morning sun, squinted, and greeted the vatos
clad in khakis, Pendleton's, knee high socks or sweet two-tone shoes.
Strolled out like you were fully dressed just in your blue boxers. Now
ese, you ain't walking in the house with just calzones. Now you got to
wear full regalia PJs. Now you strut in flannel bottom PJs to keep
your creaky knees from hurting. Now you're a grandpa, ese, and you
can't walk around your granddaughter and kids in boxers like them
olden days. Now you stroll in I-got-to-set-the-rules type of clothing
for the chamacos. Thank la diosa those boxer days are over.

Lesson Seven:  "Oh, Donna, oh Donna, I had girl and Donna was her name" . . . or "Just pull my little strings and I'm your puppet" . . . or "Oooh, I love you really I do, Angel baby, because I love you really I do, Angel baby, my Angel baby" . . . oldies East L.A. style. But goodies. Old 45s are gone now. You can't mark them up with your seña. Variations of la Lopez Maravilla. LMV. La Lopez. Y Que! Handscript in arcs, slashes in fat black markers that you can sniff for a quick high like in junior high. Blasting Art Laboe on the AM radio dial. Well, vato, how do I say this to you? But, ese, you ain't got no more 45s and there ain't no more record players. They're extinct. So now you got to listen to whatever your kids listen to. The thumping of hip-hop, rap filling your newly-minted home with angst. So, it's true, all the mierda you do as a youth comes back to you full force with your kids torturing you, just like you did to your parents. Voilà! Poof! Your la-la land is over, vato. Welcome to your verdadera days of being a dad.

Lesson Eight:  Handy man, repairman. Yep, you got in you and you didn't even know it. Remember that time you had to dismantle the old blue couch with an ax? And like a fisgón that you are and a cabezón who don't listen to directions one bit. You got your head wacked with the hacha in the center above your forehead. After that you sure learned how to fix things without completely slicing off body parts, except for your fingertip that's now long gone and only the energy exists that you swear you feel like scratching sometimes. Freaky, ¿que no? Scratch. Scratch. Now, there you are, working on one of a kind bar-b-ques. Renovate the landscaping lining the casa. New stairs to climb up to your one floor home that stretches along the cul-de-sac beneath the tagged loma—L.A. Kinda reminds you of placazos just to keep the old days alive in your family life.

Lesson Nine:    Huevón. Lazy nalga. Yes, remember, all those days that people
                thought you were doing nothing but walking the calles, sleeping in
                'til the afternoon, smoking all the mota you wanted. While in reality
                you were working as a painter of homes for low income families,
                the transporter of account stuff for a TransAm bank with big letters
                in Chinese on Atlantic Boulevard in Monterey Park, and doing the
                infamous job of cement worker. So work, work was/is in your blood.
                And would you admit the work ethic pulsated in your sangre to your
                homeboys? So, here you are twenty-five-odd years or more working
                all day, working on weekends, working at home, working . . . The point
                well, ese, you seem to possess the "I'll break my espalda" work ethic
                that your padre whipped into you with a cinto once in awhile. Knocking
                some sense into you seems to have worked out. (Of course, whipping,
                smacking, pinching, not a family trait to be passed on.) You got the
                Mexican family legacy in you. Work like a burro; live like a rey.
                And your chamacos all benefit from this. So your vato days weren't
                all a waste of time. You actually pinche worked. And who would've
                thought you live to tell you did all this?

Lesson Ten:     Simón, there are carnalas y carnales who make it out of gang life,
                la pinta, and live to tell about it. So here it is, el fin. El punto. The end.
                This, ese, is your vida. The life of a former-cholo vato loco gone to
                husbandlandia and now, a well-respected carnal.

So these are the puro chingón lessons learned from his cholo days. Who would've thought
his vato days would come in handy? ¿Que no?

# Super Queer

(Theme from *"Super Fly"* or *"Pusherman"* by Curtis Mayfield)

I'm your mother, I'm your sister, I'm your tía
    I'm Super Queer
I'm your father, I'm your brother, I'm your tío
    I'm Super Queer
I'm everywhere you look
I'm on the streets walking right by you
I'm in the office across from you
I'm in a board meeting in front of you
I'm in the classroom teaching your kids
I'm on the pew in church sitting next to you at Sunday mass
I'm everywhere you look
No matter how much you deny me
I'm everywhere you look
No matter how you silence me
I'm everywhere you look
No matter how much you ignore me
Yes, straight people, I'm everywhere you look

So look around and you'll see me    Super Queer
Hanging out, kicking back, walking around, sitting at a coffee joint
Drinking a beer at a cantina on First and Chicago Street
Drinking a limonada on the porch at Ford Boulevard and Humphreys
Sipping a margarita on a patio on Silver Lake and Sunset Boulevard
Sipping a Kahlúa on the street patio on Santa Monica and Christopher
No matter what straight boys and girls, men and women, No matter what
I'm everywhere you look
I'm in every nook and cranny you look
'Cause I'm Super Queer
    I survive homophobia
    I survive bashing

I survive heterosexism
I survive verbal insults
I survive daily beatings
I survive what you thought no human being can withstand
       I'm Super Queer

'Cause after all I'm your Amá, I'm your Apá
       I'm Super Queer
'Cause after all I'm your prima, I'm your sobrina
       I'm Super Queer
'Cause after all I'm your primo, I'm your sobrino
       I'm Super Queer
I'm your blood, and you are my sangre as well
       I'm Super Queer and I'm everywhere
I'm the president of a company, a college, a university
       I'm Super Queer and I'm everywhere
I'm a dentist, a nurse, a doctor in a hospital
       I'm Super Queer and I'm everywhere
I'm the custodian, a cashier, a lawyer
I'm the professor, union worker, a colleague
I'm the poet, artist, musician, sculptor
No matter where you look, I'm everywhere
       I'm Super Queer
Accept me, respect me, support me for who I am
       I'm Super Queer

'Cause no matter what you do I'm everywhere
I'm your abuela, I'm your abuelo, I'm your bisabuelos
I'm Super Queer who flies by you in super market aisles
I eat at taquerías on Whittier Boulevard, la Primera and el Centro

I'm standing in line with you at the bank, at the corner store
I'm everywhere you look, I'm everywhere

But you just don't wanna see me for who I am
Those heterosexist lenses you wear are blinding you
So take them off and see a rainbow world, a diverse mundo
We're shades of yellow, red, black, white, brown
In our vision, my vision you'll see there's nothing to fear
I have nothing against you, except your illogical fear
Let go of that trans-bi-homophobia 'cause it's killing the queers
We've been to way too many funerals: Brandon, Gwen, Larry
Beautiful people's lives cut 'cause society said fear, fear, fear
And I'm Super Queer ready to save the jotas, jotos, los queer, familia

'Cause after all I'm your mother, I'm your father
        I'm Super Queer
'Cause after all I'm your nieta, I'm your nieto
        I'm Super Queer
'Cause after all I'm your nina, I'm your nino
        I'm Super Queer

And when you look around without fear, hate, anger
    you don't have reason to spy on "difference" "otherness"
'Cause I look just like you and you look just like me
So take off those silly straight lentes that skew your vision
    and see the queer world for what it really is, for who we really are
We're buena gente, loving people, supportive friends, good people
You'll see that I look, am just like you and you look, am just like me
See me for who I am:
I'm your sister, I'm your brother, I'm your uncle, I'm your tía, I'm your father

I'm your mother, I'm your comadre, I'm your compadre
    I'm Super Queer
    I'm Super Queer
    I'm everywhere you look I'm there

'Cause I'm here, I'm queer and I'm here to stay
'Cause after all I have always existed in time
This is me:  I'm Kahlo, I'm Whitman, I'm Ronnie, I'm Abundito
I'm all the maricones, malfloras you pushed to the margins
I'm all the bi gente, the trans familia, you said ¡Basta! ¡A la torre!
You "blindly" choose to deny my existence, to ignore my presence
But we've always existed and I'm here, queer and will always stay
So take off that those heterosexist lenses, homophobic view
And accept me for who I am:

I'm your sister, I'm your brother, I'm your tía, I'm your tío, I'm your abuelo
I'm your abuela, I'm your father, I'm your mother, I'm your prima, I'm your nieto
I'm your sobrina, I'm your compa, I'm your comadre, I'm your sangre, I'm your familia

    I'm Super Queer!
      I'm Super Queer!
        I'm Super Queer!
Everywhere you look I'm there:    I'm Super Queer!

## Theoretical Discourse
## over "Sopa"
### (what does it really mean?)

All our lives we called it "sopa"
Differentiated "sopa" from fideo
    to estrellas or melones
labels for different pastas
titles to establish subjectivity
within the hegemonic world of pasta.
But to us, the Reyes chamacos,
    it all pinche mattered
    each limited Spanish word
    made un difference.
After all, we now knew several words
    instead of one little one
limiting the dialogue of cocinando
to the boundaries of objectivity.

As little kids we believed every word
that we were taught by our elders.
"Sopa" equaled yummy Mexican rice.
We trusted the language of adults
believed their words meant "the truth"
the signifier equates the symbol
and that's all that really mattered
within this pinche hierarchy of pasta.

We were two pochas and a pocho,
the three youngest of eight
living in the margins of East L.A.
who knew some palabras en español.
We were relegated to the confines

of the secondary position in society
in fact some of us triply oppressed.
The inner city had silenced us.
Our graffiti language scribbled on walls.

As adults my sister and I came
to terms with reality over café
and pan dulce in the cocina.
Not too long ago on a sábado
we had a theoretical discussion
about the basic noodle in life:
the foundation of the history of pasta.

Frankly, it was all about "sopa"—
          that's right—sopa and fideo.
             What does it all mean?

The yellow wall stained with grasa
stared at us or maybe even laughed.
Truth spilled out like frijoles in manteca
screaming a dolores blazing the verdad.

"Sopa means soup. You know, caldo."

"You mean it doesn't mean the rice.
How do you know?"

She, my hermana, looked at me. Shrugged.
"I heard it through the Chicana
grapevine. Can you believe it?"

"Who lied to us? I believed, you know.
Do you think Ma lied to us on purpose?"

"Nah, nah. No way. Ma would never lie."

"Shit man, I can't believe it. This is
fucked up. What happened to the truth?
Why not tell us la verdad? Goddamn,
so what about fideo? The estrellas?"

"Don't you get it? It's sopa de arroz.
Sopa de fideo . . . etc., etc. Get it?"

"Yeah, yeah. ¡Chingao! Sopa de arroz.
Sopa means caldo. That's firme. Who
would've ever known?"

"Yeah, yeah. Newfound knowledge."

From the margin to the suave center
object to layers of multiple subjectivity
the dialogue of sopa has opened like a grito
sliced the barriers of pastalandia
removed the shackles of silence
boca abierta yelling, "¡Orale pues!"

"Shit, knowledge equals fuerza. Just
like sopa equals soup. Pero you
know what?"

She nodded her cabeza up to me.
"What, esa?"

"I'm still gonna call sopa de arroz,
sopa. It's sopa to me. That other
modo. It's too damn long. Sopa is
arroz. Punto. You know."

"Yeah, sopa is sopa. And we know
what it means."

"After all, what does it all mean in
the end? Fideo. Melones. Sopa.
It all tastes good. It's all Mexican
anyways."

We raised our cafecitos to the air
clicked the copas bought from Newberry's
(Or was it La Primera store?
Anyways, we toasted.)

"To sopa. And all the fideos, estrellas."

"Simón."

# El Diablo

Beneath the onyx sky sprinkled with specks of dust
the moon's glazed eye the shade of tequila
swayed itself into a blur of borrachera
La noche's energy spilling out onto the barrio
Under the luna lay mounds of small homes
paint blistering into raw wood—termite infested
Compressed casas digging their feet into the earth
hugging themselves for shelter, for warmth
Up above peering down the loma—a sheriff's station
    keeping the poor mejicanitos in line
Reminding us prisons, jails is where we belong
    Biscailuz Center—homeboys locked up in la pinta
    Sybil Brand, a mujeres cell block for putas, locas, cholas

And below in the midst of all this barullo
He came swaggering up the calle
Guiding his way up the loma from 30 años of instinct
    He roamed the barrio as a chamaco
    Knew the alleys like his pinche home
    Age thirteen got jumped into "La Lopez Maravilla"
    Tattooed his forearm with la Virgen
    Blue ink marked the seña of the cross
      "Por vida" bled into his mano
    Vato known in the calles, to his carnales
    as a "Bien suave" pistol shooter, man
He dragged his way up along Sydney Drive
Clenching a Budweiser against his chest
Heading to the house where TV lights
Pierced out of the ventana stabbing the darkness

On 825 North Sydney Drive in East L.A.
We, my brother and I, sat in the sala
Eyes stuck on the tube blaring Tuesday night chistes
Afuera on the porch he struggled to stand still
Open hand slammed on the door once, twice . . .
    "Fuck. What was that? Hey, get the door."
Hermano mayor opened the puerta, jumped a little startled
The vato stood there behind the screen swaying a bit
    The night's shawl cradled him
Words slurred out of his mouth
    "Abel, here."
    "Nah, he don't live here, anymore."
    "Your Dad, your Dad."
    "He's asleep. Come back tomorrow. It's late."
Mouth split open into a grito, 'Too many years in the streets.'
    "I'm hungry . . . do you have any food?"
I sat on the Lazy Boy listening to the jagged conversation
Turned around and stared out the mesh of wire
A dazed glare masked his face
Blood shot eyes like the moon pleaded for help
living in the calles, the pinta, the barrio
living   "La vida loca"   stole his youth

Anger squirmed inside my venas
    Shit man, it's fuckin' cold
    Puto, fuckin' up my program
      "I'm starving. Do you have any food? Anything?"
Survival street instincts grabbed me by the garganta
Jumped up went to the front door nodded my head up to him
stared straight into his eyes checking him out

"Hey, ese. What the fuck do you want, ese?
   Abel's not here. Get the fuck outta here, now.
   Get the fuck out."
Brown eyes yearned for anything, but the calles
        ¡Ayúdame!    ¡Ayúdame!
On the unlit porch he stood there penetrating my street self
Eyes diciéndome "You know me. You know me."
Obsidian cielo wrapping itself around his silhouette
      he blended in with la noche oscura
        "I told you to get the fuck outta here."
        "Remember me. Remember me. I know your brother,
        Abel. I just live over there. On Cordova."
He pointed to his chest with his cerveza
        "Remember me, I'm Diablo . . . Diablo."


On the calles, I've seen him all my vida
Never, never once did I know his name
   "Get the fuck outta here, man. Don't be bothering us."
Slammed the puerta on him as the vato kept on gazing


Time slithered away sin vergüenza
We peeked through the window
An outline of a man lay on the zacate
      faded blue jeans   reeboks smudged with lodo
      satin stained chaqueta sangrando crimson
We stepped outside yanked, pulled him up to his feet
Pushed the pinche veterano out the cracked driveway
        "I'm hungry . . . a burrito . . ."
Tremor in his voice seeped into me
        'Recuérdate, todos somos familia.'

With his mano he squeezed the fence's railing
   "Can I have some money . . . for food?"
   "Nobody's gonna give you food. What you
    gonna do with the beer, huh?"
The vato glanced at the aluminum can
lifted it over the neighbor's rusting gate   dropped it
spewing its foam onto the ground letting the poison spill
   "There."

I remembered a mi mamá, Popeye, Blackie
A mi mamá who fed the sober veteranos with burritos
The men who slept on my neighbor's urine-tainted couch
   "Ay, Julia por favor tengo hambre."
   "Válgame, sí Popeye hay voy."

   "Mija, recuérdate. Todos somos familia."

Ran inside the casa straight into the yellow cocina
Made a burrito from dinner leftovers
   Papas, frijoles y algo más . . . necesitamos algo más

For Richard,
    a.k.a. "El Diablo"

# La Culebra de Tierra
## (Highland Park, CA)

Ronnie and Cris sit on the body of the park's homemade dirt culebra. Whisper dreams they wish their mamas could hear up en el cielo: "Amá, would you still love me? Am I still your mija?" Their words float in the arms of the spirit world. Fly across the culebra into the barrio of Highland Park.

How they lived the life of mariconas.
> On the calles men, women yelled "Fuckin' dyke!" Each palabra stabbing their
> corazones. And every evening they went to their homes with a little part of
> themselves numbed.

How they are the daughters of mexicanas who birthed lesbianas from their wombs.
> And María Socorro arose from the thick blue cielo of Zacatecas. Shedding
> the pueblo of el valle de Valparaíso from the pores of her body. She swallowed
> la chuparrosa's amor and flew to los estados into the home of her ancestors.
> Aztlán.

> Y Francisca Adelina slipped away as a niña from Hermosillo as the wind carried
> her to Tucson. One night her mamá's spirit se falleció to live with Coatlicue and
> her nana's copal burns on the altar in the recámara. Paquita left her pueblo
> in the dust of the Sonora desert to breathe blue skies.

How they are the daughters of mexicanas who never wanted to give birth to mujeres who loved women's bodies with such intensity. How their mamás as niñas were bruised early on.

> Socorro's tía slapped her with a calloused palm. And Socorro met her amor en el zócalo.
> He played el violín swaying his body to the melody. Loved her baptismal name, Julia, the
> way he loved her. Under the February pale sky, se casaron. Years slipped away and she fled
> el valle. Leaving her birth name to breathe in the desert rains.

> Paquita's papá hit her mamá on the mouth. Kept her silent with swollen lips. At night
> she, closed her ojitos, prayed with her rosario laced with flat beads to disappear like the

wind. Francisca met a boy in Nogales who serenaded her on the radio. "Ay, mi Paquita," he whispered into her ear, "soy tu Ricardo." Promised her all the libros to fill her own library. Under the June sky ripe as a limón, they married.

How they are the daughters of mexicanas who gave birth to mujeres who loved women's bodies.

Ronnie and Cris sit on the dirt tail of the serpent beneath the shade of old trees that resembled life on the edge of Avenue 57. Ronnie holds her face between her palms and cries a little for her mama, Julia, who died too young.

Two days earlier the tenth anniversary of Julia's death sliced itself into Ronnie's life. Cris rubs her compa's espalda hoping her mano could absorb all the pain.

And memories press into Cristina's mind of her mamá's death.
>    In the desert sky blooming with a girl's dream. Sand embedded its grains
>    into her skin. Underneath it molded Francisca's body and thoughts. She waited
>    for her childhood sueño of hugging her nana once more. Beneath a heavy sky,
>    she breathed in la noche's brea filling her lungs with desert pebbles and fell
>    asleep por eternidad. She flew above the montes with the wind carrying her
>    home. Left her mija with her Ricardo.

>    A year later Titina's papá died from lost love and left his only daughter to live
>    alone as a musician, painter, poet to console her emptiness.

Cris puts her arm around Ronnie's shoulder.
    "You okay, esa?"
    "Yeah."
The sky grows into a rosa. Blossoming a pink over Figueroa Street.

Months ago the park was a vacant lot studded with litter—papers, broken bottles—stabbing the ground as if slicing an artery. They sit on the rattle tip. A tierra tail laced with broken blue, yellow talavera. Clay dirt body shaped into an "S" trailing the park. Each inhales the dust of earth floating; it clings to their brown and güera skin.

Cris heard all her childhood the same ritual. "Ay, mira que linda. Tan güera como los américanos." Kissed her gently on the cheek. Rubbed her skin with agua santa. Prayed she kept her color—green eyes, light brown hair.

Each evening her mamá announced, "Ay, mi Titina. Ponte a leer." Titina loved the taste of words in her mouth. The shape of the "S." The curve of the "O." In her soft cama, she hugged the alphabet book in her arms to sleep. And her mamá wrapped herself in a romance novel. She loved the flavor of stories.

In third grade, teachers didn't believe this was Titina's mamá. How could this olive mariposa be her mom? Wondered silently 'who taught this little girl to read?' Titina turned away. Hugged her mami. She wanted to be the image of her abuela, the mujer who taught her mamá to read. And she was named María Cristina after her Nana.

Ronnie poor Ronnie labeled a gringa name. Her Tía Pancha didn't know this foreign nombre. Called her sobrina, "Ranita, ay, mi Ranita." She was named Verónica after her saint her mama loved. The saint who wiped Jesús Cristo's face with a cloth. And her mama always was tejiendo a mantel, a cobija. Needles danced in the air the way words bailaban in Ronnie's dreams.

"No juegues en el sol. Te da daño. Te vas hacer más morena, Ronnie." Spanish words cluttered themselves in her boca when she spoke to her mama. "No voy a get dark, mama."

In elementary she spoke to no one. Blushed into canela when her named was called. "Veronica." Maestras forced her to speak. She kept her lips glued and hid inside herself. In her mind, she drew pictures of stories. Listened to little girls playing Hide 'n' Go Seek. Her mama era bien linda. Ronnie wanted to be her mamá, a mexicana, who spoke español with the beauty of a mariposa.

La Culebra de Tierra grew into a recreation parque for chamacos to play fútbol, dance folklórico and paint rocks on lazy Saturday afternoons after catechism. Four levels climb the brown curves of the rattlesnake till reaching the head at the top.

They glance, scouting the place. Kids are running, booming with laughter. Four boys dodge a ball tossed at them and a little girl comes up to the marimachas.
   "I'm the gatekeeper. I mean the caretaker of the park." She stops, glances to the left screams, "Hey!" at the boys "Stop messing the place." Turns to Cris and Ronnie who smile at her. "I'm in charge." Waves her arms in a rainbow arc to show the park. "We made it. It's owned by a señora. Used to be filled with trashcans. Now it's pretty."
   Cris nods. "Yeah, it's a beautiful park. What's your name, mija?"
   "I'm Olivia. Do you wanna tour? I know everything . . . I helped build it."

Olivia tours the park, "And here," she points, "are huecos." Shows them crevices that go nowhere. "Down there we broke macetas. They were already old. We used them to make the piso." Leftover ceramics became a walkway. "Over there are pots my mama didn't want anymore." Old pottery swaddles the cactus. "Up here. This man painted a picture. He had a whole bunch of colors. I watched him. He let me wet the brushes." A mural stands on top of the layers.

Cris and Ronnie beam as this niña gives them a culebra history lesson.
   Olivia inhales. Crosses her scrawny legs, and blows words out. "Once it was an abandoned house then somebody tore it down from old age. A woman, you know, the señora, bought the land. She's an artist, you know, and made this place for us. The neighbor kids and me." The boys holler loud like a popped tire and the two dykes know someone is winning.

Ronnie remembers playing tag football as a little marimacha on the streets. Bruised arms. Knees scraped on concrete.

> Once she ran for a touchdown up the loma. She ran, ran, eyes on the flying pelota
> and ran right smack into a parked VW.
> Her knee hit the bumper.
> Her head punched the window.
> Her arms slammed into the hood.
> She caught the ball in mid-flight and that's all that mattered to them.

The little girl scampers away. And they felt their childhood disappear right into the serpent's body.

Titina and Ranita walk away . . . kicking dirt. Tossing a ball. Slugging each other on the arm.

And Olivia skips away, hits a boy and runs out of the park—La Culebra.

Ronnie and Cris sit beneath a tree. A breeze rustles the hojas and the tail of copal lifts a heavy stone from their bodies. The sun bursts into a red granada falling asleep behind the Arroyo Seco montañas. Dirt clings to their pantalones like an anointment. And the wind whispers a sueño in their ears.

> "Did you hear that esa?"
> "Yeah. That was weird. Was it a seña?"
> "Wow. I don't know. What a trip."

Las compas look at one another, nod. Ronnie and Cris stand up, wipe their jeans and walk home leaving la Culebra de Tierra for the chamacos.

# Las Montañas de Juárez

Scattered homes sleep against the rocks.
They lay across the red thunderbird
as if a mother is hugging her child.
Fall colors stain the desert like bruises:
morado, blue, verde linger in the air
and on the broken body of Tonantzín.
Each hue blisters under the heavy sol.

Imaginary boundaries divide countries
as if the dry air never crosses the border.
On a map, a thick red line leaves a scar,
reminding the people of their familias
torn between the first and third world.

In the spring, dust blows into the air
bathing la gente with the fine sand,
embedding its grains into their skin.
A sacrament blessing la frontera,
shrouding the sky in a brown rebozo:

> *To live in the desierto*
> *you have to be a cactus*
> *Holding on to the tierra*
> *Clinging with your roots*

In the evening, a silhouette of montañas
outlines the horizon of Tejas and Chihuahua.
Then the sun settles itself behind the cacti
and the sky paints an October twilight,
embracing the almas of the desert.

And below the mesa swirls el paso del norte.
Mexicanos stream the Santa Fe Puente
like el Río Bravo gliding down the canal.
Muddy water flows across the border,
cutting the land into two mirror parts,
separating hermanas like El Paso y Juárez.

Las montañas de Juárez rest among the nopales,
ocotillo, chaparral and fat boulders sleeping
in a fit of dreams like the scattered casas.

# A Xicana Theorist

In the bar she lounges near a wall of speckled mirrors
It reflects an image of a queer group in front of her
She's dressed in black jeans black boots black vest
     and a black close fit t-shirt
Her hair is short and combed back with Tres Flores
The color is brown just like her complexion
On the table is a thick ashtray and a bottle of beer
American Spirits lie next to a silver-chrome lighter
     Years ago her Apá lit his cigarettes with it:

    *He'd stand on the porch and light one*
    *pull out a ragged carton of Pall Malls*
    *cock his head to the side and inhale*
    *the blue flame into the tip of the cigarillo*
    *breathing in gray smoke filling his lungs*
    *A year or two or three he passed away—died of lost love*
    *His corazón withered into red desert sunset cielo*
       *He was such a romantic boy, always a dreamer*
         *Once he serenaded his amor por vida*
         *sang rancheras, boleros for his mujer*
      *He was a quiet man who took care of his familia*
        *He didn't dare express cariño openly*
     *And so silence is what he gave his daughter*
      *His gift to her:*   complete   utter   silence

She kept his fedora hat and Colibri lighter
   She flicks it—on, off, on, off—for a bit
    burns the tip of her finger
    memories flood her mind
    she clings to them desperately

And she squeezes the brown bottle
takes a slow drink of cold cerveza

In a hazy bar she is smoking her pack
The lit cigarette dangles from her lips
A yellow glow touches her face like a halo
   Has the catholic iglesia accepted her or
   has it condemned her to purgatory?
In the corner she is hidden in darkness
Flecks of charcoal ash sprinkle the table like a sacrament
She ponders a hypothesis over beer and cigarettes
   Xicanisma—the power of mujeres to survive
   Lesbianas—a safe space only for la jotería
   Theorists—living breathing Xicana feminist theory

Jota scholars asking themselves:

   Can queer theory be employed by a Xicana theorist
   to analyze the lives of Xicanas? Or is it simply
   white-gay-male theory exploiting the lives of women
   of color, again? Are we only fragments?

   Can straight mujeres fully understand jota dialogue?
   Or are we simply deaf to each other?

✳

A few hours ago in her office under the heavy yellow sun:

She sits behind her metal desk—a profesora
   A ph. d. in literature, american studies, history

of consciousness, ethnic studies, chicano studies
or something community-based
She bites a golden delicious apple and ponders over theory
A butch femme dialogue    can we really create our own space?
Our own xicana lesbian theory?
She is in academic trouble again   with her department
They reprimand her like a little girl lost
She always seems to be in a debate with her co-workers
She speaks her mind and they want her to shut up
'will you be quiet?  hasn't that already been done?'
Every day she fights   fights   fights   for her survival

She sits against a reflection of square mirrors
The bar is sparsely filled with yearning faces
She inhales deeply from her cigarette
The menthol warms her chest
Exhales through her nose leaving a mist of smoke
She is in a room with a few Latina femmes—beautiful mujeres
For a moment in this place she realizes her 'truth'
Here, only here, in this cantina can she be queer as she wants to be
Here, only here, in this bar she is accepted for who she is:   a marimacha
She is not a fragment here—she is somehow complete:    a whole being
She is Xicana   mujer   y   lesbiana   all at once
Across the room a mujer at a barstool eyes her up and down
whispers to a friend near her    "she's cute, ¿que no?"
She is looking in their direction and gazing at a neon light
Ideas are tinkering in her head    'Are we really safe?'

She is butch    she believes she's supposed to protect femmes
from any danger    any man who offends them and her lover understands this
She is a Xicana jota who knows the value of women
and respects this con honor

She is la mera mera macha.

She dances with the woman from the bar
She holds her gently around the waist
She leans her body closely into hers
She wants to cry and tell her she is hurt
. . . tell her she is tired of fighting
. . . tell her she feels alone and scared
She wants to heal her wounds

## Praise the Word:
### Audre Lorde is Still Alive!

I'm telling you, man, I'm telling you
       Audre Lorde is still alive!
Who would've ever thought she'd live here
right smack on 300 W. Schuster by Mesa
in the Williamsburg Apartments second floor?
Audre Lorde lives in El Paso, Texas
Who would've ever thought to look here
down at the border under this desert sun?
But I've seen her in the laundromat
  singing the blues acappella shrouded in steam
"Sister, sister, I've seen many blue skies . . ."
I spied on her peeking in through the window
listening to her sweet voice embrace each note
Yep, I've seen her here, in this border town
I know, I know you wouldn't believe it
but she's here living down in the redbrick courtyard
It was like, there she was—Audre! Audre!
Girlfriend, you're alive and well, I see    Thank you
The homegirl from New York via the Islands is back
She'd been hiding out beneath the Franklin Mountains
Writing, sketching new poems, an autobiography
to be published forthcoming in "La Mera Maricona Press"
She'd been hiding near the green cactus with fat red tunas
I'm telling you I saw her under the blue frontera sky

       Audre Lorde is still alive!   Thank la diosa almighty
She passed me down the stairs with her chingona stride
And, lucky me, she even nodded her head up to me
Said "Hello" with "Fight the Power!" vibrating in between
I knew it was her with her strut and kick ass voice

It had to be Audre Lorde rejuvenated for the pleito
   The war on dykes    The guerra on mujeres
She'd never left us    She'd been here all along
I'm telling you    Audre Lorde is still alive!
She's down here near the Río Grande waiting her time
to come back to us and spread the word
   "Poetry is political. Love thy dyke like me."
Right now, she's hiding, you know, she's keeping it low
and in between she's singing while folding her clothes
I'm telling you    Audre Lorde is still alive!

# Panocha Power!

the queer crowd screamed dreamy orgasms
books lined the narrow aisles of the store
an evening poetry reading was on its way
in the graffiti-layered streets of East L.A.
and like usual the poet was on Xicana lesbiana time
(allot fifteen minutes for each title)
they, her friend and she, were still on the freeway
on the 110 the truck was squeezing, twirling
along the narrow road that lead to the place
not sure she was gonna make the gig on time
but what the fuck she'd been late
to almost every reading in this barrio

✳

on stage she glides into the center like a subject
she read all her poesía from jota chronicles
layered with Marimacha pride
the theme: "orgullo sin fronteras"

as she read her final poema for these mujeres
her mind fluttered with thoughts of revolution
the greenwich village, the queer subculture
fluttered her mind with promise for today
and she screamed to all the jotas in the audience
to stand up for themselves and break the shackles
waving a poem in the air like a brown fist

remember stonewall—it was us las mariconas y jotos
who tore the pinche wall down into flat tortillas

not those pinche gringos who think they own our derechos
    the gay rights movement—queer nation at its best
    white gay boys taking over the scene
nah, chale man, the gringos ain't got nada to do with it
it was los puertorriqueños, the drag queens, las butch dykes
who broke every fuckin inch of the goddamn wall
      we are stonewall!!!
remember we're queer and we're here to stay
and she jumped to the edge of the stage
like there was no pinche tomorrow
only today    live for today    screeching con coraje
    Panocha!    Power!
and a lone butch from the barullo got up
wearing jota attire—black boots, jeans y white camisa
and yelled an anthem better than pledge of fuckin allegiance
    Panocha!    Power!

all the butch dykes turned around and glared at her
the poet saw the mitote reawakening hidden emotions
she prodded these stone butches to use their hard exterior
to fight for la justicia in this het controlled world
to rip the ladder of this hierarchy into saw dust
that loner butch continued her plea for vengeance
    Panocha!    Power!
every butch dyke stood up legs apart some packing some not
blue bandanas red bandanas sticking out of back pockets
yelled for all the fuckin years of lesbian bashing
    Panocha!      P-o-w-e-r!

and the poet yelped we need to take over the pinche govt.
    stand up for our rights as mariconas
and she asked the femmes to stand and scream
    this Dolores Huerta anthem con todo their might
      ¡Sí Se Puede!       ¡Sí Se Puede!
      Panocha!          P-o-w-e-r!

cuz you know they, las jota femmes, love panocha también
maybe even more than us—marimachas—nah, i don't think so
    queremos   Panocha   just as much
so the femmes with red nail polish and black dresses
wrapped in rebozos bought at the old mercado in Juárez
gritaron for their rights with all their corazones
    "we got panochas and we love panochas!"
someone in the audience chanted,  Panocha!  Power!
over and over till their voices strained like an orgasm

and then the next thing she knew from out of the corner
all the straight babes were gettin' excited, too
and they weren't gonna let their hermanas fight alone
  ¿y sabes qué pasó?  shit, mujer, you know what happened
they remembered that they have panochas también
and some carnala gritó, "babe, we gotta love our panochas!"
they grabbed their crotches, raised a fist in the air
like la virgen de Guadalupe gone loca on Xicanisma
kinda like el estilo de Ester Hernandez's lithographs
Chicana kickboxing ruca throwing chingazos left y right
gritaron with all their might in soprano voices

"ain't no man gonna control my body and mind"
"ain't no vato gonna ever keep me silent!"

and they cried for all their tías, mamás y abuelas
for all the pinche abuse they have suffered
so all the straight babes got together in harmony
someone cantó,    Panocha!    Power!
then every straight babe started to yell in high pitches
        Panocha!            Power!

and the poet sang we gotta stick together—la jotería lotería
"femmes, butches, yeah, even the straight babes"

and the poet stared straight into crowd
        cheering and clapping with joy
con cariño, hermanidad y comadres por vida
she smiled and nodded her head in approval
the entire room was standing and chanting
        Panocha!      Power!

yeah that's the way it's supposed to be
mujeres together—loving and supporting each other
        none of that backstabbing shit
        none of that gringo power trip crap

the poet shouted one last grito de dolores
para her mamá and all the women who came before her
who carved the path and created this red road to follow
every one stood on their feet and threw a grito con orgullo
        Panocha!             Power!
        Panocha!!            Power!!
        Panocha!!!           Power!!!

Gracias . . .

# Texas Twilight on the Border
## (El Paso, TX)

Cobalt glazes the sky into a blue earthen bowl
Peaks of white clouds flower up down up
into round edges silhouetted on desert mountains
Heavy blues to sweet papaya orange press against the ridges
squeezing the red tunas, the brown espinas of a nopal
Then the evening drapes a black cortina on the montañas
as if it is a cardboard cutout behind a luminous light
And dreams, hopes flutter above the river canal
across the borders that slice families in half

She gazes through the steel-wire fence like a prisoner
Little squares running diagonally into the dry night
crisscrossing her mind with wire and sliced estrellas
A beam of light outlines the tip of montañas negras
A deafening glow immersed in a white circle
like the migra spotlighting someone crossing the fence

And Cristo Rey waits for eternity, erect on the west tip
arms stretched, ready to bless and the shadow even longer
during the day gives false hope to the poor, to Mexicans

She stands behind the black pen and journal—a poet
lacing strays of ink on bleached sheets of paper—
 Her canvas, Her art, Her drawings, Her stories

The white-marble man stands under the blistered sun:
open eyes facing the blueness of the north
open eyes facing the redness of the southwest
open eyes facing the brownness of the desert

and resurrected in this sandpaper desierto   a statue
exclaiming to the cielo, the people, "I absolve you . . ."

And she wonders for what: "We did nothing wrong."

# El Año Nuevo:
## A Tamale Evening Ritual

### I. 1976

In East L.A. the aroma of tamales filled the cocina
    Corn hojas lined the mesa in the yellow room
    Masa spilled onto the brown-smudged tabletop
The speckled black pot on the stove simmered con cariño
All night las mujeres worked cocinando—sipping Kahlúas
The hombres sat in the sala tomando Tecate, Negra Modelo
looking at Dick Clark's "New Year's Rockin' Eve" special
Both corners of the house the año nuevo stirred    hope    desire
    more money for food    more dreams to keep them alive

The entire casa steamed with New Year's Eve
I wandered outside to the cuartito for a moment
In the small room, a sink huddled by the door
As a little girl, my job was to swirl and rinse
the dry corn husks in agua tibia 'til tender
And I stared at the wall—yellow paint peeling
A December draft snuck in between the slabs of wood
I shivered as if the wind planted a seed in my body
The golden tips of the curlicues trembled from the music
El violín sang Norteñas as Apá slid his calloused fingertips
along the neck of the 1920-something string instrument
Outside the door way above the green zacate
    an orchestra of blinking estrellas hummed
Y la luna llena swayed in the onyx sky
conducting a harmony between the stars and the earth
Over the stream of música, I heard my mama
Her voiced shimmered—each note floated into the thick night
cantando just like Lola Beltrán on New Year's Eve

## II. 1986

On the 31st of Diciembre, 1986, balazos streamed across the noche
Fourth of July fireworks flashed the sky, popped in the air
Each precious unused firecracker saved for this evening
And the only clamor in the house blared New York
The TV was tuned onto channel seven ABC
Over the years now only three mujeres of the house
        kneaded masa     steamed tamales
and inside me fear of time struck a dissonant chord
Maybe I knew    Maybe I knew this would be the last time
I saw her face, her body tired from so many years weighing on her
As my mama walked slowly into the sala, I feigned tiredness
"Ya me voy a dormir . . ."
"Buenas noche, Ronnie."

As I lay under the covers hiding my face, it slapped me
Time—I couldn't stop the twenty minutes
      Counting down:  20, 19, 18, . . .
Tears streamed down my cheeks in the darkness
On the other side of the green cortina, my sister and mama talked, laughed
I squeezed my face into the red rose hair-dyed almohada
Time—I couldn't stop the fuckin' time
      Counting down:  . . . 3, 2, 1
The clock chimed twelve times
They screamed, "¡Feliz Año Nuevo!"
Faintly through the green curtains, I saw them hugging tightly
Amá boomed with joy, "Válgame, ya pasó otro año."
And I cried and cried yearning to slip out of bed to hug her
   "Mama . . . Mama"
My words fell asleep into the pillow

III. 1998

Twelve years had floated away into the murky river
Tamale making evenings only a memory like steam from a pot
In '87 she died after 10 years of fighting: drugs, hospitals, medi-cal
I was just a girl blossoming into a mujer who was lost

And when '98 came into my life like an offender
        a full load of toxins released itself into my body
On Schuster and Mesa, the doctor spilled the words
as if precious water had no meaning
in a desert of a hundred degrees in midsummer days:
        "Your hands are shaking; your eyes bug out.
         Your heart stammers like a jogger."
         (he thought this was funny, smiled.)
         "You got Graves disease."
I stood there in the suddenly cold room and stared at the white wall
"At least you don't got cancer . . ." his words lingered in the sterile air

Graves disease entered my life like an inherited family "gift"
(a thyroid ailment that strangled every inch of me)
And I remembered my mama had endured—seven ugly diseases by age 60
And I have one, only one, following her path
One illness strangling my corazón—pounding it at 100 beats per minute
pushing it out the brown cavity of my heavy chest
slipping, throbbing in my clogged throat
My body hair will shed like a rattlesnake leaving her skin
All night long my mind will be sleepless, an insomniac
And my brown long hair will fall like grains of fine sand

## IV. 1999

El Año Nuevo stabbed my vein with its blunt needle
In my father's house, the navidad tree shimmered
    A rainbow touched the green-flowered wallpaper
Tamales no longer simmered in the yellow cocina
I sat alone in a room with no familia around
waiting for el Día de los Reyes to arrive
Over the years, everyone fluttered away like chuparrosas
leaving this house empty of laughter, cariño

Enero days slip away into the blue desert sky
(my life a wisp of a dream in time)
I wait in the hair salon on Mesa Avenue near Cincinnati
And the older Japanese woman asks one more time
"Do you really want to cut your hair? All of it?"
I nod, "Yes, cut it all and leave only one inch of hair on my head."
She takes the scissors, the entire place breathes in once and watches. Everyone frozen.
She snips slowly right to left and my head feels light    weightless
I whisper to myself over and over inside:

*I will cut every fine strand of brown hair*
*like a curandera offering a prayer to the desert wind*
*a sacrament for la diosa—la Virgen de Guadalupe*
*blowing each strand among the ocotillo, chaparral, lagartijas y culebras*
*praying, hoping this female disease does not kill me*
*like a mi mamá—seven diseases ravaged her body*
*And I hope, pray for a cure in my lifetime.*

# This is my Angela Davis Poem

Prelude:   So everyone, listen to these fine profound words

So this is, people, this is my Angela Davis poem

The poem that sings the times I never met her

The moments of "in-between-the-years" where I missed the woman

The woman who coulda changed my eighteen-year-old politics

The woman who I coulda bowed to out of respect at thirty-four

The poem that shouts my eighteen-year-old sueños, my naiveness

The poem that screams, "Why didn't you tell me she was in Toronto?

I missed Angela Davis, again; twice in my little old life time; why me?"

So, here it is, here it is. . . . This is my Angela Davis poem


*People! People! The prison system is another form of slavery*
*It is an enforced binary system where the master-slave dichotomy is reflected*
*Can you believe it, that today we still live in a "master-controlled" economy?*
*Yes, people, the prison system is simply another form of slavery*


I listened to those words come out of her mouth and fill my ears, my soul

And my boca went "What! Oh, my diosa. We live in a slave society; we never left."

I listened to those words from this powerful woman speak of today's Black society

Speak of today's reality for Latino and Black young men entrapped by prison walls

You name it: San Quentin, Folsom, Las Tunas, Super Max "rehabilitation centers"

And my mouth just plopped on down my chin onto my "Free the People!" t-shirt

I just couldn't believe, couldn't believe what I was hearing on that spoken word CD

It hit me the way cops beat Black kids, Mexican kids, Salvadoran kids, poor kids

with their palm-smoothed batons down in Compton, North Long Beach, Maywood,

City Terrace, Boyle Heights, HP, South Central and anywhere else we are at

And I thought, 'Why? Why have I not met this wonderful, powerful Black woman?'


So people, here it is, my Angela Davis poem—the beginnings of my formative years

The beginnings of my woman of color, my dyke of color feminist self ideology

Back at San Diego State University flyers were posted up everywhere on campus
The 1970 photo: "WANTED By the FBI—Interstate Flight, Murder and Kidnapping"
It flapped around the brick buildings, corkboards, walls like little rainbows dancing
down in the Student Union, up in Hardy Tower Hall, near the Academic Skills Center
She came strolling onto the campus to spout political anthems from the ground up
And I, my poor little Chicana blossoming self, knew not who this powerful woman was
And I, like a sappy young self, headed off to class and learned Intro to Anthropology
What a f-o-o-l I was, to think I missed the most dynamic woman politicizing the world
Oh, how could I have missed Dr. Angela Davis speak at San Diego State University?

They say, she was a powerhouse talking politics that afternoon at four-something
They say, she riled up the packed lecture hall with the urgency to "Fight the Power!"
They say, her words inspired the audience to stand up to speak our diverse voices
They say, her ideas, her beliefs, her passion invigorated the student population

All I'm saying is that I cannot believe that I missed her speaking engagement
I cannot believe now that no one, no one told me the importance of Dr. Davis
I cannot believe now that no one, not even a Chicana sister told me straight up
"Miss class, girlfriend; skip it and learn from the ground up. Learn from Davis."
I cannot believe now that no one, no one said such a thing to me to educate me
Oh, how I could not have realized the importance of this afternoon lecture
Oh, how I could've been a different, politicized young Chicana from el barrio
Oh, Angela, if I knew, realized this significant event, I would've skipped class

So this is my Angela Davis poem saying, Power to the People! Power!

*People! People! The prison system has enslaved our youth*
*The majority are young Black men, Latinos, Native men*
*and White poor working class men locked up on a daily basis*
*We must examine the governmental system that perpetuates itself*

*We must examine and think of ways beyond this binary system*
*I am speaking of, specifically, the transgendered, bodies locked in prisons*
*Look how this narrow system labels sexuality then imposes it on prisoners*
*We cannot subsist at this level in this binary system that perpetuates hate*
*We must tear down the system link by link that enslaves our youth*

So, there I was, right smack in the middle of northern maple leaf country
And learned through the queer grape vine, after the fact, that she was—here
Angela, Angela, oh, Dr. Davis, I missed you, again, in this frozen Capitol city
How can that be, how can that be that you slipped on by? And I never knew
They say, the feminists at the Toronto Women's Bookstore it was overflowing
They say, there was a line heading down King Circle at U of T just to get in
They say, I probably would not have been able to get in to see her anyways
They say, these words to make me feel better that I missed Dr. Davis, again
But I'm saying, I could have called out, found her in the crowd and screamed
"Dr. Davis! Dr. Davis! I'm a Chicana dyke from East L.A., from el barrio"
And she would've, I truly believe it, let me in the house because I existed
because I was only one of two Chicana dykes living in Toronto from L.A.
And my feminist self was in shock that I missed the iconic, powerful mujer
How could it be, how could it be that I missed this dynamic speaker?

So this is my Angela Davis poem:   Power to the people, Power!
                                   Power to the queers, Power!
                                   Power to women of color, Power!

*People! People! Artists like Gloria Anzaldúa are at the center of imagination*
*We must understand that feminist artists always further revolutionary change*
*We must understand that they encourage us to imagine what is possible*

*We must understand our interconnections, our existence on the border*
*We must understand our intersectionality: race, sex, class, and sexuality*
*We must not eradicate the voices of activists, the voices of Native women*
*These women challenge and provide a new way of looking, existing in this world*
*People, people, the artists are existing in Nepantla, the entremedio,*
*the middle bridge between two spaces and creating new ways of being*

So this is my Angela Davis poem in honor of her, in honor of her work
This is my Angela Davis poem sharing her wisdom, her words in print
Dr. Davis saying to the people, to all the communities, to the world
"We must think of other ways to exist, to be in this world.
We must practice methodology of all Women of Color feminisms."

And I say, "This is my Angela Davis Poem" and I dedicate this poem to her
In some queer way, if I had not missed those Woman of Color lectures
In some queer way, if I had not missed my eighteen-year-old induction
this poem of politics and formulation of jota feminist self would not exist
and I say, "This is my Angela Davis Poem" would not have existed
and it must and it does 'cause of all those missed lectures of a powerful mujer


Finale:    So everyone, I hope you listened to those profound words
           So everyone, I hope you practice these beliefs in your lives
           So there it is, there it is. . . . This is my Angela Davis poem.

           Thank you, thank you, Dr. Davis.

# The Fields

The sun dipped behind the smooth blue horizon
and the light dimmed just as twilight settled in
nudging itself gently beneath the cool cover
Up north I gaze across rows of purple uvas
The acrylic sky darkens and speckles glint
and the evening wind smells of grapes, sea

A mi Apá was born outside the skirt of a ripe field
lechuga, fresas groomed the green hem of Denver
Francisca, a mujer indígena, chaparrita, his mamá
She, the shade of café con canela, he, a tinge of mezcal
and she christened him a name mirroring Navidad
This son, her son, was born on this side of the river
past the Nueces, past the Sandía Mountains
past millions of brown piñones draping the land
like many others, his name never recorded on paper

A mi Mamá nació in the land of nopales, prickly pears
and an old chaparral tapete lay on the packed tierra
Her mamá, someone's daughter, forgotten, lost
She, a forgotten name, birthed her daughter in an adobe
and she named her the sound of dolor and dulce: Socorro
This child, this girl, was born on the espina of Zacatecas
This child, this daughter, her life a fissure in turquoise
This child, this mujer, mi mamá, lives in our corazones
Like many mujeres, her life rarely recorded on paper

Some say Pancha, mi abuela, never, never once shed dolor
She named her mijo under the cielo's shimmering opal star
In the 1920s, los Reyes trekked "home" to nopal desert
In San Antonio, his name scrawled on crinkled paper
     his birth year, day of birth smeared in black ink
He is a smudge in this país reflecting his name, his birth

Some say my mamá's mamá nunca lloró ni amó su hija
In the crisp madrugada, dew silenced the land of el valle
and her tiny scream pierced the blue air like a chuparrosa
At age 23, she crossed el Río Bravo into a foreign tierra
In El Paso, her esposo scratched Julia on "green" papeles
and Socorro flew back home to a flattened mud home

Out on Scott Street the fields shimmer deep reds, blues
I gaze at the spine of the old turtle mountain's back
The wooden patio overlooks vines blossoming vino tinto
A silhouette of curved, rugged edges lines the crisp sky
Everything is so beautiful out back in St. Helena's yard
I think of mi Apá, a mi Mamá and remember their lives

90 years living in a country where he stumbles in English
A mi Papá, now each step a temblor, dreams of corriendo
A man who never really knew his malflora daughter
His watery brown eyes cradle memories of México antiguo

And my mama 60 years strangled her heart, her alma
A mi Mamá never, never knew me as a grown woman

Her corazón suffocated from manteca and sadness
Her kidneys drained her alma into red sunset flores

I gaze at the estrellas blooming into white orchids
I stare out at the rows of lush vines swaddling grapes
And I script their lives in watery ink like un Río Bravo

# Wine Country

Dusty plots stamp the ground like the people
Threaded lines made of sticks absorb warmth
Each field row holding green, purple bundles

The poet strolls past the old barn house
It is all splintered wood, rusty tin roof
She passes over the dry arroyo bed

At the corner of Pope Street and Main
she sees Mexican men waiting to cross
    the street, themselves, el río
And she wonders, Do they work the field?

✳

In Delano the UFW called strike against California grapes
Dolores Huerta chanted, "¡Sí Se Puede! ¡Sí Se Puede!"
The big grape owners labeled her, the Dragon Lady

And Javier, a brown queer boy, worked the lines
like many Chicanos, he believed in raza unida
like many Chicanos, he became pesticide mist

And Chávez, the son of migrant workers
in a peaceful protest went on a hunger strike
And everyone remembers his name

＊

In downtown it is a clear distinction like wine
between the owners of the vineyards, merlot
and the workers of the vineyards, smashed uvas

Across from the Natural Food and Health store
the Mexican men wait for the green light
And the poet stares at the men who mirror her

She strolls by and they lock each other's eyes
Their brownness binds them in this country
Halfway across they nod "Bueno" to each other

And she wonders, Do they think she works the field?

# Migrant Worker

## I. A Field Worker

The heavy sun bakes her skin with dust and sweat
rows of dirt lines itself on her tender neck
like the green fields her Amá y hermanos work on
picking the seasonal lechuga, cebollas o lo que sea
Her espalda the shape of the moon's grimace hurts
The sun a sledgehammer pounds rays of heat
slicing through her camisa burning her skin
Sweat wraps arms, legs and beneath her clothing
Her bare skin glistens into enflamed canela sticks
boiling in an olla of agua melting Abuelita's chocolate

En la pisca everyone reeks of raw onion y sudor
*at age sixteen she missed her quinceañera*
She glances at her manos with sore fingers and blisters
*at age ten she missed her classroom teatro*
Keeps her body bent down pulling the seed that blossoms
*at age twenty she tucked her dreams in her falda*
Remembered life would be different en el otro lado
She laughs to the wind that blows warmth down her neck
Funny how she can now laugh at a young girl's silly thought
She yanks her sueños from the fine soil dusting her mano
Wipes her hands on her sides and some topsoil clings to her
Some flies in the ocean breeze back to the land of her home
Some glides in the cool harvest air back to the cold city
And it lands east of the puente in the middle of Los Angeles
And plops itself in a dream of a little girl who dreams stories

## II. Migrant Professor

The white room smells of books and copier ink
Dressed in charcoal slacks, blue portfolio dress shirt
I wait for the Director to enter the white-gleaming office
wait for the interview for a teaching job in academia

And the red haired woman types away on the computer
eyes glued to the screen and idle conversation beginning
Little words tossed here and there in the hygienic office
Then she thrusts a hard line out and her words linger
I listen to the navaja-sharp words hanging in the air

"So you're an illegal alien."

Suddenly, the hot air expands into globs in the office
The secretary grins to the computer and no one else
The stench of stale English grammar books permeates
The copy machine drones mangled noise, deflated notes
I look at her and words get stuck inside my garganta
like a cracked bone caught in my throat choking me
and my mouth opens slightly spewing warm air

And the Director calls me into her pale blue office
smiles a business woman's hello-welcome to the department
and in her germ-free office half the size of the dean's
She spills a pool of words onto the clean table

"You know the personnel director said, well, that . . .
called you an illegal alien. Can you believe that?
You know, they don't use that word up here."

She smiles; I nod my head and say nothing to her
and she asks me, "So when can you start teaching?"

✳

After twelve years of university schooling
it slapped me that I am the same woman picking
plucking, yanking, pulling vegetables for American tables
that I am the same brown Mexican woman picking
plucking, yanking, pulling fruit for American dinners
I am the Chicana college English instructor whose plight
partly reflects the Mexican woman working en la pisca
I do not have her pay nor do I have all her struggles
But I am more *her* than any gringo in my life
After twelve years of university education
what I've learned is that in this country—Canada
I am the immigrant, undocumented or not
and I get treated like mierda almost like she does
After twelve years of university schooling
I see myself and have realized in one brief moment
I am her and she is me—a migrant worker—
I teach part-time in square plots of scattered colleges
She works fulltime, earns half the minimum pay en la pisca
I am a "professional" migrant worker in academia
And she is a migrant worker who is invisible en el fil
I am her and she is me—a migrant worker—
We share the same roots; we share a tangled life.

# The Queer Retablo Series:
## Butch-Femme Dialogue

### I. The Kiss

In a black vestido, she leans over to kiss her,
a short-haired woman wearing creased Dickies,
a slick-white dress shirt, and smiles to herself.

### II. Custom Frame

Gold trimmings line burgundy-framed edges
crowned in pine green bougainvillea swirls,
mount an evening, a girl to boy-girl kiss.

### III. Snapshot

Black-white still image presses a tender beso.
Las malfloras, gaze in, sit facing the center
and a friend, the camera mujer, shoots la foto.

### IV. The Lips

The lips linger partway in the warm air
and the soft static passes between them.
They lean in more and the photo snaps.

### V. The Shoes

Spit-shined black men's zapatos waxed and
black-velvety tacones wiped down for la noche.
Estrellas glint, obsidian sky gleams like shoes.

## VI. The Energy

Around them rainbow particles burst open flying,
friends dance salsa, play '80s music, sing "Tainted Love."
Their jota lives thrive in their red home, their red altar.

## VII. The Dialogue

The lovers whisper words swimming in the cool air.
They float over the barrio, over the glistening lake.
In Silver Lake before the kiss, she says, "Te quiero."

# The Alamo Motel

The sky hugs the land as if the blue can touch the face of the earth. The sun beams white light directly into the eyes and burns them. Fat rays bake the skin under 105-degree heat blasting the ground. The people stay hidden in homes, buildings, cantinas on both sides.

And in the Alamo Motel, Modesta waits in the plastered lobby. On the carpet, paint flecks like sprinkled sea salt absorbs the air. It reeks of American Spirits from gaudy tourists who layover for the night:

> Sometimes they get stuck from Austin heading to Tucson, sleep the night
> Sometimes virgins come to lose themselves in the motel and be free
> Sometimes newcomers from el otro lado stay to hide from la migra

And Modesta in her bleached apron cleans their messes, learns their lives.

From desert sun-up painted with black-red summer silhouettes to the red-black evening, she sees the blue bus pass by. Once an hour on Alameda Street to Valle Verde. Across the thick Texas sky, it slices the heat and disappears into a mirage; it streams by the slouched motel, and passengers see the 1950's décor: script letters wading in a warped plastic sign. The border sun's drained the hues into dusty ash like the March winds.

She's been working over the border since she first arrived to this side and like many who came to El Chuco, she was only passing through, buying time, just enough to make a little money to head on up to el Norte. Chicago, she once pondered, she should go and visit her baby brother and like many passing El Chuco, she never left the grainy desert city. The bordered horizon down in the Lower Valley became her home.

She's seen many things over the past 20 years in the motel rooms.
Some she remembers and others have flitted away like a pebble skipping across a dirt road.

> Once there was a guy who stood in this smoked filled room. Typing, typing away on the old Smith Corona. Chunky black typewriter, the kind you have to slam down the keys to stamp a letter on the onion paper. Smoked three packs a day. Drank coffee, a pot and a

half. Modesta came and filled up his carafe. In the deep blue mañanas, she made cinnamon coffee for 'em. She was young then. In her twenties. Long blue-black hair and wore it in a trenza. She'd come in and pick up after him. The writer. He'd be clucking at the machine. Some cowboy story. The lies of King Ranch County, the Alamo revolt and how Santa Ana came, stole Texan land. The lies of the gringo cowboy to make himself feel better. Sometimes he read to her while she picked up after him. And she did love the way he described the land, Hueco Tanks, Franklin Mountains—the southern tip of the Rockies peering over at Mexican country. Chaparral tumbling on the highway. Ocotillo blossoming red floral for just over a week. In the desert evenings he'd go eat dinner at Luby's or Furr's. Have himself a good American meal—fried chicken, mashed potatoes and small cup of corn. Then sometimes he'd go down over the border. She'd seen him stroll out to these places. Once she'd seen him out at the tianguis near Guadalupe Church sitting on a cobblestone sarape. He seemed an odd fixture, towering over the Mexican vendors. Eating a cup of elote. He saw her, simply nodded his Stetson hat. She knew she'd see him tomorrow. He'd been there a month. Follow the ritual: clean the room, hear the cowboy drawl reading aloud. One morning Modesta crossed Oregon Street under the open sky cracking lightening. She passed a small hacienda pressed flat from the sun, shrunken from age. Saw a brass sign above the doorway. 1910 Mariano Azuela wrote his novel, *The Underdogs*, here. She strolled to her blue bus stop near San Jacinto Plaza—the place where alligators used to live. When she got to work, like the rest of 'em, the writer was gone.

In the Alamo Motel, Modesta cleans after the patrons and learns their lives from skeletal remains. She sits in the lobby on her afternoon breaks. Watches the hourly bus slice the thick Texas sky, splashing it a blue wash. The motel sits alone out on Alameda waiting for the city to spread its wings to this edge. And Modesta stares out the lobby, dreaming of a young woman's life.

And she imagines the sky hugging the land as if the blue can really touch the face of the earth.

# Socorro

the sun waits in the mid blue cielo
and in the nuzzle of heat, spring rises
from sidewalks into the soles of shoes
she paces up to sydney drive dreaming
picking a special route home every day
in her morning journey to hammel school
she counts the cracks on the ground
one by one jumping over the soft crevices
crosses her fingers passing under an arch

*Every evening you fed me stories*
*I learned the gift from you*

by midday she wanders home from school
moving her lips like whispers in church
mumbling her stories in two languages
acting out the scenes like a mime
she travels up eastern   right on folsom
left on sydney till halfway up the hill
the mailman passes her carrying a leather bag
she opens the driveway gate   stands still
waiting for the mailbox's mouth to open wide
like jaws to swallow fat letters, scrawny cartas
to snap shut on a mailman's finger for lunch
she stares at him as he stuffs the box

*Poems seep into my sueños*
*Similes, metaphors, personifications*
*linger in my everyday thoughts*

she opens the metal box   pulls out
an airmail envelope stamped en méxico
that crossed la frontera like a legal citizen
it is as thick as onion skin breathing
in the warm winds of desert montañas
black ink smears like a tear en mano escrita
   "Socorro Reyes"
the bold letters written in a harsh scrawl
mimicking the lives of her family's sufrimiento
crooked letras scribbled in a child's hand
she holds it up to the sun as if a sacrifice to dios
as powerful as her mama's rosary on the altar
laying near la virgen in the recámara

*Your memory lives in my cuentos*
*You exist en tinta negra forever*

she takes the piece of paper inside
walks in the sala screams  ¡ya vine!
her mama emerges through the cortinas
she beams and gives her the letter
asks her the question engraved forever
   Mama, who's Socorro?
the "r's" tumble out against her teeth
her mama smiles    touches her mija
rubs her hija's small shoulder
healing her wound that would come
   Ah, ¿pues quién sabe?
   Ahora, no es nadie.

her mama laughs con gusto
    Ay, Ronnie en México me llamaban
    Socorro. Nomás es un nombre.

*In my dreams you speak to me*
*tell me all the stories I need*
*answer all the questions I ask*

she walks away says nothing
only accepts her mamá's answer
as if it made perfect sense
her mama goes to the cocina
ronnie hides behind the cortina
watches her mamá sit at the mesa
carefully she peels open the carta
she glides out the two thin papeles
reads each word as if it tastes
as rich as mole as sabroso as menudo
like the méxico of her girlhood
her mamá savors the flavor of each word
in her boca to last her a lifetime

*I read each poem  story*
*giving birth to its life*
*become each breath  action*
*like my tías   my primos*
*who preformed each cuento*
*in the middle of the sala*
*singing a tradition en español*
*The rhythm of life in Zacatecas*

ronnie steps outside in the backyard
sits on the big red lawn chair
faces the skirt of the white house
dreams of names floating in spanish
the peach tree blossoms in pink
and the apple tree hovers behind her
Socorro    the name flies away in the air
as if a chuparrosa carries it back home
into the depths of the thick blue sky
somewhere in the heart of el valle
the valparaíso of her mamá's name

# Winter Desert/Summer Glacier

All day glaring-white domingo, snowflakes like tiny kisses caress the barren pine, the green roofs, and the wind-chill crackling ground sprinkles a soft-blue-white drift smooth as hot sand grains in the desert heat, mirroring summer café con leche glaciers that plaster the rolling ground into a light brown sea, waving reflections of tierra up down up down. And clear crystal grains glint in the blue-frost air in the center of a winter storm in T.O. Centimeter after centimeter piles onto one another rising, rising slowly like a mercury thermometer in summer or falling down, down in deep glacial air crisp to the touch. The way a Chihuahuan sandstorm covers the sky a deep brown hugging the curves of Juárez and the northwest edges of El Paso like a white out on Highway 27 in winter. Each tiny pebble flying in the blue-brown flat grounds shrouding the tierra with a new-layer mirroring a fresh sheath of white that embraces High Park, Roncesvalles, Wellesley. Each coat wrapping around the north or southern edge like a cobija in white-tan shade; blanketing stone ridges, fat rocks and shallow crevices with minute gems shimmering up towards the sky's gray clouds squeezing tightly as if holding its breath or an open blue sky bursting with a loud smile that envelops that entire land to the north, to the south. The land's marshes in the northern crevice and the deserts in the southern tip shine with nature's fragrant-majestic beauty seen in winter deserts, summer glaciers outline sprinkles of maple leafs covering the deep-blue-white of snowstorms or brown-green ocotillos sitting under summer blazes over a hundred baking the skin; each haven in the center of two polar extremes, and within this white-brown pebbled canvas, the cielo colors each day with Northeast-Southwest hues, shades of blue-purple evenings over the edge of the Franklin Mountains, beyond the edge of Lake Ontario; and the poet admires nature's sketches of everyday landscapes and savors each precious drop of memories, of all her homes—Northeast and Southwest.

Epilogue

# East L.A. Poet

The Mexican lime tree towers in the desert backyard blooming flowered lives
And the white-marbled sun blasts a fat ray on the dry zacate, leathered nopales
This is my childhood home where I grew up hearing my mama sing "Paloma Blanca"
This is my childhood home where I grew up listening to my papa playing el violín
This is my childhood home: beneath two jails, below the loma, by the freeway

The nopal hangs out by the old wired fence, a chicken coop and a cut red wood spleen
thorned palms yearn upward; knotted back carries cacti branches like a green poncho
And my Apá wearing his tattered straw hat cuts new growth, cuchillos the tender nopal
At 80 or 90 he is inventive estilo a la brava; found ways to make up for limited mobility

> He ties a cuchillo to an old pole, reaches up
> and saws at the new cacti tendrils. They fall
> on pebbled ground, hang on lower ramas. He
> stabs them. Pulls them in like the viejito
> and the sea, estilo Zacatecano; he brings in
> his fresh catch: nopal.

In an hour or so the air thickened—homemade nopalitos wafted in the yellowed cocina.
In the kitchen, I studied literature, wrote poetry, typed poesía on my Smith-Corona
And manteca stains spread greasy marks on my textbooks, notes like a forbidden traveler
Once I took my poems to the Vincent Price Gallery, in a trembled voice I asked a writer

> "Can you read them?" Brown eyes blinking in awe; my god, I was so young

The front nopal's sprouting over 100 tunas, sweet prickly pears nesting, in all its glory
A señora at El Superior on Rowan gave him the plantita in a tin can, smiled a gold diente

> "Este nopalito va a dar miles de tunas. Vas a ver."

And in the back jardín, desert cacti grow as if they have found Tenochtitlán in East L.A.
On that same parking lot, he saw her, la diosa de Mexica, de México waiting in all her gloria

> La Virgen de Guadalupe spoke to him, asked for tres frijolitos and left him in awe

In the foreground yellow flores glint petals to tierra, to the lizard roaming the concrete wall
Years ago peach trees blossomed pink buds in spring time from the cariño de mi mamá
She spoke to her plantas as she worked her jardín and bathed them in her gardener's love
Now purple flower bundles like bouquets adorn the foot of the cacti sitting near el cochinito,
the old frijol pot sits on a rock, and a rusted trash can lid hangs: a painting of maguey

Sydney Drive's been my home for forty-one years on the same block, a family home for fifty
My mama, Julia Socorro, died here in 1987 in the newly painted pink room on an autumn day
In the garden backdrop a Día de los Muertos statue stands near the rib of mama's red lawn chair
Now we celebrate life with marigolds, skeletal figurines—ceramic or paper mâché—cradling
death on an altar like la catrina palms up waiting for a veladora to light its way back to el cielo
As a tomboy, I ran and ran around the blue house in my super duper tennies from Zody's
From the side of the casa grew rosas, I'd rub soft tierra like ceniza on my brown chubby piernas
And I'd come running to my mama; she'd be lavando ropa in the cuartito and I plopped myself
Like the roadrunner I announced, "I'm here. Mama! Ya llegué from trabajo." And I beamed cariño
And inside the cuartito's open-mouthed puerta, she shook her head, smiled Válgame

Las tunas now blush crimson against a blue sky whitewashed and left out on the clothesline
And my Apá snipped two prickly pears to savor el Valle de Valparaíso, the jugo awakens him
In his home state, the land a sarape of cacti, ocotillo and brown espinas pinch the cielo's shawl
And his mama y papa's, mis abuelos, adobe casita nestled itself beneath the desert montaña
On North Sydney Drive, the Reyes live near a sliced "montaña" hugging frogland, rabbitland
and they made a home near a tiny mountain swathed in shrubs, and flowered cacti, Zacatecas

Pink, red rosas line the front fence where white carnations graced our home's welcome mat
La chuparrosa skates the wind, stops midflight, hovers near petals, and drinks the flor's miel
like me—I am a marimacha crossing la tierra, el mundo and always coming back to East L.A.
We, my sisters, brothers, and papa, sit under the shade; an old arbol that's lived with us for years
The green-yellow helicopters scan the land and the wind lathers us in a cool summer breeze
Years ago in the '70s we'd play "Chopper Chopper" up the shrubbery loma cradling buildings

the fire station, Smokey the Bear, the practice range; on Saturdays we'd hear the pop, pop
And my mama on hot summer days made rainbows for us with her magic and a manguera

Under the sombra, we enjoy good company and pláticas de cosas serias, chistes y good chisme
The barrio sounds chime in every so often: "¡Elote!" "¡Raspados!" "¡Huevos!" "¡Fruta!"
Cars whisk by the way la chota skims by homes peering in like ladrones of people's minds
In my youth, gunshots flicked the brea sky and the training began: how to survive, to exist
I can tell at times from instinct where the shots came from by listening to the cuete's pops
    "Ooh, shit. Hear that. Down on Eastern and Fisher. Listen."
And I've seen my brother's back nicked like razor bites from the whacks of a black baton

And the nopales absorb the sol's warmth like un abrazo from familia, from a longtime friend
And now I live in the humid cuartito: sketch poetry, cuentos from el barrio, from my home
"La Paloma Negra" trumpets from the untrimmed sala the shade of atole, agua de maíz
On Saturdays his ritual, he watches "Sábado Gigante" like a smooth shot of golden tequila
The años have passed the land, gente like white carnations blooming, withering, dreaming
And still this rosado-stucco home thrives with three generations' energy, cariño, sangre
    I am East L.A. like the people, the calles, el barrio.
    I am the East L.A. Poet.

# Biographical Note

Verónica Reyes is a Chicana feminist jota poet from East Los Angeles, California. She is proud to have attended Hammel Street School, Belvedere Jr. High School, and Garfield High School. She earned her BA from California State University, Long Beach and her MFA from University of Texas, El Paso. Her poems give voice to all her communities: Chicanas/os, immigrants, Mexican Americans, and la jotería. Reyes has won AWP's Intro-Journal Project, an Astraea Lesbian Foundation Emerging Artist award, and was a Finalist for the Andrés Montoya Poetry award. She has received grants and fellowships from Vermont Studio Center, Virginia Center for the Creative Arts, Ragdale Foundation, and Montalvo Arts Center. Her work has appeared in *Calyx*, *Feminist Studies*, *ZYZZYVA*, and *The New York Quarterly*.